Secrets In the Suitcase

Stories My Mother Never Told Me

Stories by Molly Greenberg

Reflections by
Rosalie Greenberg, MD

authorHOUSE®

AuthorHouse™
1663 Liberty Drive
Bloomington, IN 47403
www.authorhouse.com
Phone: 1-800-839-8640

Published by AuthorHouse 12/03/2012

ISBN: 978-1-4772-8209-0 (sc)
ISBN: 978-1-4772-8210-6 (hc)
ISBN: 978-1-4772-8211-3 (e)

Library of Congress Control Number: 2012919493

ALTHOUGH I HAVE PUT the stories together, there is no question that this book was written by Molly Greenberg, my mother.

I strongly believe that she would support my words.

Contents

Acknowledgments

Many people helped me make this book of my mother's words a reality. I must thank my close friend, Lois Tigay, for getting me started on this journey by helping transcribe my mother's stories. Thank you, Natalie Elman, for your assistance with the title, even when the book was still just a concept in my head. I am indebted to Sunny Yudkoff for her masterful translation of my mother's Yiddish poem. I am grateful to Sandy Marino, Claire Guadagno, and Faye Cunningham for their unflagging encouragement and support. As always, thank you Jacqueline Tull; without you, my day-to-day life would be so much harder, and finishing this effort would have taken much longer.

My parents' longtime friends from Brooklyn, Judith and Israel Shiloff, were helpful when we met to talk about my parents' experiences after arriving in America. To Tony Hauser and Max Mermelstein, I applaud all your hard work to keep knowledge of our common Skala roots alive. Max and Clara Mermelstein, Malcia Rothstein, and Leo and Susie Karpfen were all so kind in opening up their homes and their hearts to me in discussing memories that I know at times were very painful. I am indebted to Susie for her input with the manuscript.

Without my dear friend and communications director Marisa Tuhy's persistence and belief in me, this book might not have been completed. To her family: Jim, Tess, Alice, and Nora, I thank you for your patience and generosity in sharing your wife and mother's time and talents to help me with my project.

My sister, Evelyn, and I are beyond thankful to Molly Burack, who taught our mother's creative writing class at the West Orange Jewish Community Center. By appreciating and encouraging our mom's creative efforts, Molly provided her with a safe way to finally let out her innermost feelings of pain and torment.

I am eternally indebted to my husband, Soly; my sons, Ryan and Matt; and my sweet dog, Asta, for reminding me every day, just by their presence, how blessed I am.

Last but not at all least, I have to thank my parents for giving me such an amazing sister, Evelyn. Her limitless love, support, and strength in everyday life is more than any sibling could hope for. Helping me with this book in different ways—accompanying me on visits to our parents' old friends, spending hours going over the minutia in the manuscript to make sure our mother's words were clear and right—made it easier for this book to exist. Thank you, Sis, with all my heart.

Bashert

BASHERT (בַּאשֶרט) is a Yiddish word that means "destiny," "fated," "kismet," or the phrase "what's meant to be is meant to be." I often heard my mother utter this term when I was a young child growing up in Brooklyn. She would use it to explain the reason why something happened—whether good or bad. It was her way of helping me make sense of things that on occasion defied reason.

Looking back at my life, I realize that the concept of bashert has served me well as an important calming and grounding belief. As you will soon learn, the discovery of my mother's stories and the subsequent creation of this book fall under that same guidepost.

It was the spring of 2007. My older sister, Evelyn (aka Evie), decided to remodel her kitchen. Rummaging through her drawers, cleaning before the destruction of the old kitchen and the planned construction of the new one, she came across a few items that she couldn't quite place. One of them was a small key that was hiding in the back of a narrow cutlery drawer. After a few seconds of thought, she decided that it probably belonged to something insignificant and long gone. After all, had it had meaning, she'd never have left it in such a hidden place.

With that, she put the key in the middle of the kitchen table, with all the rest of the odds and ends she continued to discover.

Once she got started in the kitchen, she was so driven that she decided she *had* to take on the basement. The children's old toys, her old books from college, and her spouse's neglected shoes from his youth were all sent packing.

In the midst of this cleaning furor, she found a vaguely familiar small suitcase. It was a black metallic American Standard case, probably as old as her thirty-four years of marriage. It had been her husband's gift from my parents when he finished law school. She pressed the appropriate tabs repeatedly but nothing happened. Looking more carefully, she realized that this particular black case required a key. Thirty years later, where was this key? She didn't remember. Evelyn brought the case up from the basement to throw out with the other discarded items she piled together. It was then she remembered the key in the middle of the kitchen table. Well, she thought, there was nothing to lose. Evelyn got the key, and to her astonishment, it slid right in. The case opened effortlessly. No, it did not contain gold or diamonds or jewelry but one-of-a-kind items that were of inestimable and infinite value to the right people. In this satchel were the stories of my mother's life. Any adult child would be excited to make such a discovery. The difference here is that my mother never really spoke about her childhood to my sister and me as we were growing up.

You see, my sister Evelyn and I always knew that our parents were originally from Poland and survivors of World War II and Adolf Hitler's attempts to make the world *Judenfrei* (free of Jews). My father had aunts and uncles who came to the United States before the war, who made it possible for him to bring his family to America to start a new life.

Growing up in Brooklyn, New York, we were familiar with some of my father's family: our great aunts and uncles, my father's brother, Ben, and our various cousins. We were told a little bit about my dad's youth in Europe. But our mother never really spoke about her background. We knew the outlines of her life—she was an orphan by age three, raised by her five older siblings. Unlike the rest of her Jewish-looking family, she was born with blond hair, blue eyes, and a small nose. Her looks were the key to her survival as she lived through World War II. By leaving her childhood home and assuming the identity of Mary, a Polish *shikse* (a non-Jew) she was able to survive. Under this guise, she was able to obtain a job as a Christian maid/nanny for a Polish family that had no idea of her real identity. Her non-Jewish exterior helped her secure ongoing shelter, at least until her true identity was discovered. She then was able to go to another city and not be discovered.

After the war, my mother returned to her former hometown, Skala Podolska, to learn that most of the Jewish people had perished, including her five siblings. Within a few months, she married my father, Sam Greenberg, another Skala survivor who was ten years her senior.

The couple spent the next few years in a displaced persons (DP) camp, called Fohrenwald, in Germany, where my older sister Evelyn was born in October 1946. They stayed there until January 1949 when they received approval for immigration to the United States to join my father's aunts and uncles, who were residing in New York City. Less than two years later, in December 1950, I was born.

Growing up in Brooklyn, I always felt there was an unspoken horror and pain that existed within my mother's heart, whose details I did not know.

In 1984, after my sister's two children, Jonathan and Elysia, were born and I gave birth to my first son, Ryan, my parents made the difficult decision to move to New Jersey from New York City to be near their grandchildren.

It was only a few months later that my mother was diagnosed with breast cancer at age sixty. Ever the fighter, she spent the next ten years courageously battling the illness's recurrences and progression, through different surgeries, multiple courses of chemotherapy, and radiation treatments.

It was during this time that she joined a creative writing class for seniors at the local Jewish Community Center (JCC) in West Orange, New Jersey. There, through the encouragement of her gifted teacher, Molly Burack, and her supportive classmates (including her spouse, my father, Sam), she was finally able to muster the courage to confront the pain of her past.

During these years, she won two awards for her writing: The Legacies Award (1992), a national competition sponsored by the Jewish Association for Services for the Aged, and a creative writing award by the Authors/Writers Network at Montclair State College. In addition, some of her stories were published in local newspapers during the Jewish holidays. It was through the process of writing that my mother was able to experience a bit of inner peace. She took great pleasure in visiting local elementary schools and reading stories about her childhood to the children. They in turn wrote very sweet letters thanking her for sharing memories of her youth with them.

Mom passed away in June 1995 from complications of her long-standing struggle with cancer.

A few weeks after her funeral, we packed her possessions and put some in storage at Evelyn's home and mine, and left some with our father when he moved into a senior citizen's facility.

Dad lived more than a decade after Mom passed away. In his last three years, he developed a post-stroke dementia and spent time living with both my sister's family as well as my own.

As my children got older, I began to have more time to think about my parents' lives.

I thought about looking closer at my mother's stories, assuming there existed no more than twenty in total, and maybe getting some of the pieces published.

Once my sister told me about her fortuitous discovery of my mother's forgotten writings, I knew that finding the key and the suitcase were the signs that I *had* to work on this book. Or put another way, as I like to view it, my sister's discovery meant that this book was truly *beshert*.

Rosalie Greenberg, MD
August 2012

From Her Peers

MY MOTHER'S CREATIVE WRITING class created a book of stories that they dedicated to her. It began the following way:

This volume is dedicated to the memory of our beloved classmate, Molly Greenberg, a Holocaust survivor who found her voice as she opened her heart to us.

Molly Greenberg was a born storyteller. Eagerly the group would await her tales, some heartbreaking, others humorous, always poignant. In 1992, she won a prize in the nationwide Legacies contest for writers over sixty. On several occasions, she read her stories and spoke with grade school children about her own childhood in Poland and her life during the Nazi regime.

Molly Greenberg was a light in our class ... gone too soon. May her memory be a blessing.

Teacher Molly Burack
Creative Writing Class
JCC West Orange
1996

CHAPTER ONE

In Her Own Words

What Writing Does for Me

SURVIVING THE TERRIBLE ORDEAL of the Holocaust left me with an abundance of very disturbing emotions: anxiety, fear, anger, and despair. Everything seemed to be tangled and locked up deep inside of me. From time to time, these emotions would emerge to the surface, pressing to be released. I could not do it. It seemed to me that talking about my innermost feelings, about the conflicts, would tear me apart. It would be like disrobing and showing the world my open wounds, which never healed—the naked depths of my soul. I was afraid that people would not understand me. I was not sure what their reaction would be, and I did not want to be hurt again.

When I started to write, I found an outlet. By putting them down on paper, I opened a new door through which I could release my feelings. Somehow, when I read back the words that I write, they seem to lose some of their severity; they diminish the impact of the spoken word; they do not hurt so much. Being able to express myself in writing makes a world of difference to me and also to my children. Since I could never answer all the questions they asked me, as I did not want to hurt them, my answers were always short and unrevealing. "How come we have no grandparents, no aunts or uncles or cousins? What happened to all of them?" Now I can put on paper, for my children to read, the whole story of my past and my lost family. Just as important is telling the world of the horrible experiences, of the mental and physical torture that millions of Jews and I suffered at the hands of the Nazi murderers.

The Truth: To Tell or Not Tell?

"MOTHER, WHY?" I HEARD my daughter, Rosalie, asking while turning away from the computer where she was typing one of my stories. Although she didn't finish the sentence, I knew what she meant. I finished it in my mind, "Mother, why didn't you tell us?"

What could I say? That it was my pain that I carried within me, and that I feared hurting them by revealing my past? Or was it my guilt? I felt guilty depriving them of the very precious things that other children had: a grandmother, a grandfather, an uncle, an aunt, a cousin, or just a relative.

I tried to be all of that to them. I devoted most of my life to them. I did everything I could to compensate for the loss they suffered. I tried to grow with them. When they were Brownies, I was a Brownie leader. When they were Girl Scouts, I became a Girl Scout leader. When they started college, I went to college so they would be proud of me. I would be equal with other parents who were born here and went to college.

But was doing all that enough or even right?

Wouldn't it have been fairer to tell them the truth so they would not wonder, asking themselves where they came from and where their roots were? Did I wait too long, dismissing the questions they so often asked about my family by simply saying, "They all died"?

Now they are grown mature people. And when they read my stories, they wonder and ask questions. Why did I conceal the truth all the years they were growing up? I hope they understand why I did it. But do they approve of it? Do they feel I was justified in denying the truth? I often wonder.

I do know I was lucky that in spite of the conflict, my two daughters grew up to be well-adjusted, decent human beings.

My Teacher

PAINFUL MEMORIES AND TERRIFYING nightmares of what I witnessed during the Holocaust have haunted me throughout my adult life. A tangled web of disturbing emotions, such as anxiety, terror, anger, grief, and guilt, created a wound in me that time could not heal.

Then one day, something wonderful happened. I was introduced to a very special person. She opened a new door for me, a door into a world of writing. She encouraged and inspired me by giving to me the most important gift: it was the belief in my ability to write.

Somehow when I put my feelings on paper, they help diminish the rawness of the wounds. I owe that to my teacher. Sometimes I feel like she would take my hand and lead me from one week to another, from one story to another. She is the most understanding person you would ever want to meet. She never criticizes. She corrects you. She always finds something worthwhile even in the most poorly written story. She is extremely intelligent and well-read. I admire her. All I can say is, "Thank you, Molly Burack, for having me in your class."

CHAPTER TWO

The Early Years

(1924–1939)

The Background

MY MOTHER'S FATHER, WOLF Itzig Feuerstein, was born in 1853 in Galicia, part of the Austrian Empire. Today this area in Eastern Europe is known as the Ukraine. This region has a long history of shifting borders and rulers.

In 1876, at age twenty-three, Wolf Itzig married Rifka Schmirer from the town of Mikulin'ce. Together they had five sons: Nachman (born 1880), Samson (1886), Binem (1889), Süsie (1892), and Szloma Schaje (1896). Their youngest child was born in Gusztyn, one of a few small villages that surrounded the bigger town of Skala Podolska.

Rifka died near the turn of the twentieth century. Subsequently, her five children emigrated from Gusztyn to places unknown.

Wolf Itzig remarried. He and his new wife, Toby Pohorilles, had six children. There were three boys, Rubin (born 1911), Mendel (1917), and Leib (1919), and three girls, Roza (1914), Elka (Helen) (1921), and Malka (1924), or Molly, my mother.

The family owned a liquor store and bar called a *kretshme* (an inn) in Gusztyn. They did not serve wine or any special drinks, only beer and vodka.

Wolf was seventy-two and his wife forty when their youngest child, Malka, was born on December 22, 1924. Within a few months, Wolf passed away. His passing made life even harder for the family. Rubin, the fourteen-year-old, as the eldest male, assumed his father's position and ran the inn. But over time, the hardship only increased. In 1927, when Malka was not yet three, her mother passed away from tuberculosis.

Malka and her five siblings became orphans and were left to fend for themselves. Roza, herself only a child of thirteen, had to assume the role of the mother for the younger siblings. Life for the Feuerstein children was difficult. Malka's childhood was punctuated by a myriad of deprivations: nights of going to bed hungry, a sparse supply of clothing, intense loneliness, and the wish to have the attentive, protective mothering that was impossible to expect from a sister only ten years her elder. Though poor, the family was able to survive on their own for a decade in Gusztyn, which was a small, mainly Christian village

Over the course of the 1930s, the Nazi Party and anti-Semitism insidiously gained a strong foothold in Poland. This had to affect the Feuersteins, as they were one of the only two or three Jewish families in Gusztyn. Due to escalating ethnic tensions, the family made the decision to move to a nearby shtetel, Skala Podolska, when Malka was eleven. Skala Podolska was a big town that had over two thousand Jews. Most of the families made a living from the crops that they grew in the field. Again, the Feuerstein family struggled and barely made ends meet. One brother worked at a mill. Although life was hard, Malka was delighted to be in a place where learning and education were valued. Academically, she thrived and dreamed of a future of higher learning. Physically, she was quite thin and delicate-looking and somewhat plagued by gastrointestinal problems (which years later was diagnosed as ulcerative colitis). Malka was very close to her family and somewhat private about her personal feelings with peers.

I Remember My Mother

I REMEMBER ONE LARGE room. In one corner stood a bed, and opposite it was a daybed. It looked like a wide, long wooden bench with a removable cover and four little legs. Daytime, it served as a sitting place, and at night the cover was removed and inside there was a straw sack that rested under a featherbed and two pillows. It became me and my sister's bed. As it was kind of narrow, we each slept on opposite sides. In the middle of the room stood a large table on which the family ate their meals. In another corner was the stove. The stove was built from bricks and had a black tin door. The top of the stove was a large square made of cast iron. Next to it stood the oven, also made from bricks. The inside of the oven was shaped like half an oval, but the very important thing was the outside top of the oven. It was built like a little box with room enough for one person. I remember fighting over it during the cold winter nights. Each one of us wanted to sleep there since it was the warmest spot in the house. I never got a chance since I was the youngest of six.

There was no wooden floor in our kitchen. It was a clay floor. I remember every Friday, my family put clay on it and whitewashed the stove and oven with lime. I don't remember much about my mother working in the kitchen. Only one incident is clear in my mind:

It was a nasty, foggy fall day. I was almost three years old, sitting on the floor, playing with the pots and pans. My mother was standing at the table, kneading some dough. I got up and asked her to put me on a chair next to where she stood. She just looked at me but did not move. I started to cry. Suddenly, I saw my mother bending down and then sliding to the floor. I did not understand what was happening. Was my mother trying to play with me? When she did not move, I started to scream. My brother and sister ran in from the outside, picked my mother up, and put her on the bed.

I ran over to the bed, crying, "Mama, Mama, take me. Hold me." But she did not even look at me. She just turned the other way. That was the last time I saw my mother. I was less than three years old.

The next day, early in the morning, my oldest sister, Roza, woke me up, dressed me, and said she would take me to our neighbor's for the day. Before I left, I ran over to my mother's bed. It was empty.

When I returned home the next day and did not find my mother,

I became hysterical, asking, "Where is she?" They told me she went to heaven. "But why?" I asked.

"She was sick and had tuberculosis," my sister responded. I was sad but initially accepted it.

Then one day while playing with some children, I had a fight with my best friend, Susi. She turned to me and said, "My mother told me that your mother did not want you. She did not like you. She turned away from you just before she died."

"You are a liar and so is your mother. My mother loved me," I yelled, but I felt a terrible pain inside of me. I ran home crying hysterically. I told my family what happened. They tried to explain to me that my mother loved me very much. That last day when she knew that she was dying, she could not bear to leave me, her baby. She could not face it, so she turned away. They were right. But nevertheless … I was left with a scar forever.

M.O.T.H.E.R.

Six simple letters, M.O.T.H.E.R., form a beautiful word, *mother*, the most precious, loving sound in a child's life. A mother's love and care is true, unselfish, a pure treasure. Lucky are the people who can share it with her.

Unfortunately, I am not one of them. I had no mother or father. I grew up an orphan, the youngest of six children, an orphan by age three. I wanted to have a mother. I needed one. I yearned for one.

But it was not until I got married and had children of my own that I fully realized what I had missed: a tight embrace through the night when troubled by pain, a bedtime story, a good night kiss, the sight of her loving face when I woke up in the morning, me playing in the bathtub while her soothing hand cleaned and caressed me, a warm embrace and kiss as she was seeing me off to school, her staying in the window waving good-bye, assuring me she will be there when I return.

As I grew older, she would, with the touch of her gentle fingers, comb and braid my hair, and then stand me in front of a mirror, her eyes shining with love and pride. Then she'd tell me how lovely I looked. Finally, she would stand by my side with tears of happiness in her eyes ... her baby was getting married.

I know, Mother, that you would have done all of these things for me, but you could not. You died too young.

The Dog

THOUGH I WAS ONLY five years old, I knew who the neighbor was talking about. I was told the story over and over. At times, our old Aunt Miriam, who lived in a little village in Poland, took care of us. She was a very good-hearted person. One rainy night, my aunt heard a noise like a cry or whining of a little child or an animal. When she walked outside, she saw a dog with a bleeding paw. Since it was a very small village, everybody knew every dog by name. This one was a stray. That did not stop my Aunt Miriam. She took him in. "Why don't you put him down?" I heard our neighbor yelling at my older brother, Rubin. "He is a nuisance. He does not see or hear well. He just roams around and messes wherever he pleases." My brother just looked at him and did not answer and walked into the house.

I helped clean his wound and gave him some food and let him out. After that, the dog would come every night to get some food and then run away. One day, my Aunt Miriam became very ill; she suffered from tuberculosis. She had to stay in bed in a separate room since there were no sanitariums at the time. When night came, the dog came to the door. My sister gave him some food, but he would not touch it and would not leave. He started to howl and scratch at the door where Aunt Miriam lay. She heard him and asked my sister to let him in. He lay down next to her bed and stayed there the whole time, except to get some food and go outside when nature called. Aunt Miriam died three months later.

The first week, the dog just sat with his head up, howling, refusing food. After a while, he seemed to calm down and started to eat. We decided to keep him, and he became a part of our family. We called him *Khaver*, which means *friend*. After a few years, Khaver got old and had three strokes, one after another. Deaf and partially blind, he just walked around the neighborhood, getting lost from time to time. We always found him and brought him back. The neighbor's complaints did not bother us, as we would never put him down. He was a devoted and loyal friend. One day, he walked away and we could not find him. Two days later, a neighborhood boy found him lying under a bush. He was dead. It seemed he had had another stroke. We cried and missed him like part of our family. We had lost a devoted and loyal friend.

Malkale:
Youthful Memories

WHENEVER I PLAY WITH my grandchildren, who are between two and seven years old, I see the abundance of dolls and toys, from the simplest to the most advanced mechanical inventions. I frequently compare their childhood with my own.

As I played with the children of peasants, our toys were simple and primitive. The most popular ones were pots and pans, beans and walnuts. You cannot imagine how exciting it could be for a small child to listen to the sound of beans while throwing them into that pot and spilling them out again and again, or watching the walnuts rolling all over the floor. The most thrilling thing was playing in the mud, making mud pies and building castles.

Being a girl, I wished I had a doll, although I had never seen a doll before. I could visualize how a doll looked, something soft and cuddly, something I could hold and love. I pestered my sister for a long time until she finally agreed to make me a doll. She made the body from rags. Then she cut pieces of wire, covered them with cloth, and made them into arms and legs. For the head, she used a small potato covered with a baby sock. She used two black pieces of felt as the eyes and one red piece as the mouth. The hair was made from strings of golden threads. Finally she sewed all the parts together, and that's how my first doll, Malkele, was born. I loved Malkele very much. I pretended that she was my baby. I bathed her and fed her; I hugged and kissed her and told her all my troubles. I played with her all day and slept with her at night.

One day while I was playing outside with Malkele, it started to rain. I ran into the house, leaving her behind. When it stopped raining, I rushed outside to get her. She was soaking wet. It took a few days until she dried out. But something terrible happened to her.

When I woke up one morning, I smelled something bad. I realized it was Malkale. I decided she must have gas. When my family discovered the smell, they told me Malkele must go. "It is not gas," they said. "It is her head—the potato got rotten."

I pleaded and cried, throwing tantrums, but nothing helped. Malkele was tossed into the garbage. I was very upset and lonely, impossible to please. No matter what my family offered me, I only wanted Malkele. From a happy little girl, I became a miserable little brat. When I think of this incident, I realize how important toys are in a little child's life. Toys broaden a child's imagination and give a sense of security and happiness.

Forbidden Fruit

I GREW UP IN a traditional and very religious Jewish home. We strictly observed the Jewish laws and traditions, especially when it came to *kashruth* (Jewish dietary laws). We were taught what we were allowed to eat and what was forbidden.

As we lived in a small village among Gentiles, most of my friends were not Jewish. It was very hard for me to not be able to do things that most of the other children did. The hardest thing was that I was never allowed to eat in my friends' homes.

I remember one time when I was about eight years old, I was playing with one of my non-Jewish friends, and when dinnertime came, she asked me to stay for dinner. I knew that I should not, but I just couldn't resist the smell of the spaghetti sauce, so I stayed. I ate only the spaghetti without the sauce. I figured that the spaghetti by itself was not *treyfe* (unkosher). When I came home and told my family about it, they got very angry with me. They said that I did a terrible thing. I sinned. Although the spaghetti was not treyfe, it was cooked in a non-kosher pot so it became treyfe and naturally forbidden to me.

I felt very unhappy and scared that G-d would punish me. I decided that, after all, I did not do it on purpose. I just forgot about the pot, and it is G-d who made me forget, so it was His fault. In that case, I was not guilty, and I couldn't be punished.

As childish as this reasoning was, it seemed somehow to stick in my mind. Whenever I do something that is forbidden, I think of that incident. The only difference is that when you are an adult, you can't reason things out so easily because logically you can't just dismiss the wrongdoing by blaming it on someone else. So when you are guilty, you are just stuck with it!

In Poland

THE VILLAGE GUSZTYN WAS surrounded by woods and ponds. The little houses of mud, bricks, and straw roofs looked like gigantic mushrooms surrounded by shrubs and bushes. Each house had two large rooms. One served as a kitchen, dining room, and social room. The second room was for sleeping. No matter how many people were in the family, they all slept in one room, usually two or three in one bed. The worst thing was that there was no bathroom in the house. A little shed behind the house served as a toilet. Taking a bath, however, was a big hassle. We had no water or heating system. We had to carry the water from a well, heat it on the stove, and pour it into a basin that served as a bathtub. There was one grocery store, which sold the most necessary things, such as sugar, oil, flour, and coffee. There were no clothing stores; people made their own clothes from the material they bought in the city.

We had no television, movies, or even a radio, but we did have a Victrola in our town. The man who owned it would put it out on his lawn every Sunday, and whoever wanted to listen had to pay a *groshen*, which is equal to a penny. I still remember how excited I was when I heard it for the first time; I just could not understand how a box with a big tube could sing.

Nobody had a car; we traveled by horse and buggy. It was a lot of fun, but one time I almost got killed. Small children were not allowed to ride the horse and buggy by themselves. Being nine years old, I thought that I was a big girl, so when nobody was looking, I got into the buggy and started to ride. The horse must have been thirsty because he ran straight to the pond outside the village. As he ran into the pond, the buggy turned over and I fell into the water. Luckily the water was shallow, so I just came away with some bruises and mud. This incident left me with a fear of horses that I still have to this very day.

In Poland (A Poem)

When I was nine, when I was nine
My greatest wish was to have a bike that rides.

When I was nine, I had my first date.
We went for a walk along a lake.

When I was nine in Poland, I played
The princess who kissed the frog,
And changed him back into a prince.
And in the Purim play, I was Queen Esther.

When I was nine in Poland,
I milked a cow and
Saw a calf being born.
When I was nine, I churned butter
In a wooden butter maker.

When I was nine in Poland
I saw for the first time a car.
It was riding through the streets of our village.

When I was nine in Poland,
I walked to school—twenty kilometers
Every day, there and back.

When I was nine, I shared a bed
With my two sisters,
And once when I was angry at my sister
I put a frog on her side of the bed.

Helen

"Molly, get up." I felt someone shaking my arm. "I want to show you something." It was my older sister, Helen, the nature lover. Helen was eleven, two years older than me. She pulled me outside and, pointing in one direction, she said, "Look at that beautiful sunrise." Beautiful, indeed it was. Like a big red ball of fire, the sun was slowly emerging from the far east.

"It is going to be a hot day," Helen said. "Let's call some friends and go on a picnic to Lucy's house." Lucy lived at the outskirts of the village. Her house was surrounded by a lot of trees and big grounds. But most important, her mother had a wooden washtub, which she filled with cold water so we could jump in when it got very hot. The picnic was a lot of fun. We played games, sang songs, and recited some poems that we had learned in school.

Suddenly, a slight darkness started to slowly creep in, making us feel very uncomfortable. It wasn't a storm or anything like that. The sky was perfectly clear, dark blue, without a trace of clouds. Panic-stricken, we all ran home. When Helen and I got home, we found our older brother and sister in front of the house, looking up at the sky through a piece of smoked glass. They yelled at us to go in the house and not look at the sun because we could become blind. It was too late. We had already looked. We saw half of the sun covered with a shadow, which looked like a black patch to me. I was petrified, but at the same time thrilled by the physical phenomena—the first eclipse I had ever seen.

Mud

THE ROADS IN OUR village were dirt roads. There were no cars; the most we saw were two to three cars a year. When that happened, it was a big thrill. We would all run after the car. The big excitement was trying to keep the chickens and the dogs away from the street and then chasing the car to try to catch it.

When I was nine years old, my family decided to build a new house because the old one was falling apart. They created a big basin and filled it with water, mud, and straw. A few people went in it and started to knead with their feet. When it was kneaded well, they would take a wooden mold, fill it with mud and make a brick. They would leave the mud brick in the sun to dry, and from these bricks they built a house. I was a little girl and was not allowed to go in the basin. But kneading looked like so much fun, so one time when nobody was around, I went into the basin. Before I knew it, I was over my waistline in mud. The more I tried to move, the deeper into the mud I got. Very frightened, I tried to move the mud with my hands so that I could make a path that I could go through. After a while, I became totally covered with mud. I still could not get myself free.

As I started to cry, suddenly my brother Rubin appeared. He grabbed me with his big hands and, with a look of annoyance, pulled me out of my mud prison. He told me a mud basin was like quicksand and not a place for a little girl to play. He scolded me and said that I should never do that again. Believe me, it was so frightening it's a lesson I never forgot.

A True Friend

ONCE I HEARD SOMEONE say, "If you make one true friend in your life, you are very lucky." How true that is. I was one of the lucky ones, for I had a true friend in my life.

I was eleven years old when my family moved to Skala. It was summertime. At first, I was very lonely. I was overwhelmed to see so many Jewish children whom I did not know. The summer passed, and I enrolled in the public school. As I was a good student, many of my classmates tried to be friendly with me. I felt they did not seek my friendship but wanted my help with schoolwork, which I gladly gave. There was one girl, Lucy Steinman, whose father was a doctor, which in a small shtetel carried a great deal of prestige. Lucy became my good friend. She did not need my help since she was brilliant. We liked the same things, read the same books, and kept one diary between the two of us. We even liked the same boys!

When I was twelve, I developed pneumonia, coughing nonstop. Because my mother had died of tuberculosis, I became very upset and was frightened that I too might die. I went to see Lucy's father. After he examined me, he said that he was almost sure that I did not have tuberculosis. Somehow, I was not convinced. I became depressed and tried not to mingle with people, and when I coughed, I walked out of the room. I tried to eat lunch in private.

When Lucy saw what I was trying to do, she invited me to have dinner at her home. As we sat at the table and her mother started to serve, Lucy got up and said, "Mommy, I am not so hungry. I will share supper with Molly."

When the soup was served, Lucy took her spoon and ate from my plate and then shared the potted chicken, dipping her roll into the gravy on my plate. I will never forget that potted chicken, even though every bit I swallowed was salted with my tears. I realized what Lucy was doing. She tried to show me that I did not have tuberculosis or any other contagious disease. She was ready to share with me, whatever it was.

I had a true friend, but no more. Lucy was killed by the Nazis. I mourn for her like I do for my own family. May she rest in heaven since she helped provide a piece of heaven here for me on earth.

Sukkot

As the holidays came closer, we, the children, got more and more excited. Holidays meant so many things to us. First, a new wardrobe. There were suits for the boys, new shoes, and shirts. If someone was lucky, he even got a tie and a haircut. The girls got new dresses, slips, shoes, and ribbons for their hair. Then came the time for everybody to take a bath. Taking a bath in our shtetl was a treat more than a routine. As we had no water or heating system or a bathtub, we had to carry the water from the well, and then heat it on a stove and pour it into a tin tub. Very often, two kids bathed together at one time, to save time and water.

Whenever Rosh Hashanah came, we were all ready, dressed up and walking around like peacocks, waiting for the big happening—the supper. Often through the year we had been poorly fed, but when the holiday supper came, everybody indulged in the most delicious food. The menu was usually gefilte fish, chicken soup, turkey, and homemade cakes and cookies.

The next happy holiday for the children was Yom Kippur. While all adults were fasting and praying in the synagogue for life, health, and happiness, we, the children, were having a feast, eating everything we could get our hands on.

Then came the happiest holiday of all: Sukkot. Helping build a *sukkah* was a lot of fun and very exciting. Eating in it was a real picnic. I remember our special sukkah. We built it from our sticks and straw. The roof, which was half open on top, was covered with corn stalks and grass. As we sat down to eat supper in the sukkah, we heard a banging noise from a nearby roof. The sounds were coming closer and closer over our heads. Suddenly, something gigantic leaped down on our super table, frightening everybody to death. We soon found out what had happened. The goats liked to climb on the low straw roofs of the little houses. While roaming around on the next-door roof, one goat must have smelled the fresh grass on top of the sukkah. Not realizing that there was no real roof, he walked straight into the opening on top of the sukkah and landed on the table, right on our food. At first there was chaos and a lot of confusion. After a while, everything quieted down and we had a lot of fun playing with the goat. All the food had gotten messed up and we had no supper that night. But we did have fun.

Kitty

MY FAMILY RAISED CHICKENS, ducks, and geese, and we also had a cow, a horse, a dog, and a cat.

As I had very few friends who lived close by, I mostly played by myself or spent my time with the animals. I loved to watch how my sister milked the cow and how the chickens laid the eggs. I even watched how a calf was born. When the calf grew older, I played with him. I loved the animals very much.

Most of all, I loved the little kitten, which I got for my eighth birthday. Gray with a touch of white under her chin, she was beautiful. I called her Kitty, and I loved her very much. I taught her all kinds of tricks: how to turn over and play dead, how to take a bow, and how to beg for food. Just one thing about Kitty upset me. When we played outside, she would chase the tiny birds and then eat them.

As Kitty grew older, we noticed that she would disappear every night for a few hours. When she returned, she refused to eat the next day. She was getting bigger and fatter each day. My family decided that Kitty was going to have kittens. I was overjoyed. I could not wait for them to come, but time passed and nothing happened. Kitty got her appetite back, but no kittens. We could not understand what was going on.

Then one day a neighbor from the farm next to us came to visit and told us about his troubles. It seemed that somebody had been stealing his tiny baby chicks. For a while, this was happening every night. But as soon as the chicks got bigger, the stealing stopped. He could not figure out who could have done it—possibly a rat or a skunk. But we knew. It was Kitty!

Now we knew where she was disappearing to each night. Because we all loved Kitty so much, we could not just let her go. Still, we realized we could not keep her on the farm. We gave her to a relative in a nearby city, where there were no baby chicks or birds to catch. I missed Kitty very much.

A few weeks later, while coming home from school, I saw my sister running toward me with Kitty in her arms. Kitty had come back! This was amazing because usually only dogs find their way home—cats don't. But as I said before, Kitty was a very unusual cat.

We just could not give Kitty away again. We decided to keep her, but she could not walk out of the house. She became strictly a house cat—which made me very happy!

Aunt Fiegelle

SHE WAS VERY PETITE, very tiny. Everything about her was small: her hands, her feet, her body, even her facial features. The only big things about her were her black eyes and a mouth to match. She always wore a long black skirt with big pockets, a black blouse, and a babushka on her head that she never took off. She claimed that the babushkas kept her head warm in the winter. "And when the head is warm, the whole body is warm," she would say. In the summer, the babushka protected her from the sun and wind so her body kept cool. That was my aunt. Her name was Feige, but everybody called her *Feigelle the Koyekh* (which means "the Mighty").

Feigelle was not an ordinary person. She was very special. She was the biggest bargainer in our shtetl. Everybody liked to go shopping with Feigelle. They were sure that with her around, they would get a bargain.

When I was twelve years old, my Aunt Feigelle took me shopping to the market. "You're old enough to learn how to shop," she said. Our first stop was at a fish stand. The fish on the stand looked very good to me; some even looked alive. But my aunt had her own way of seeing things. She held her nose and started yelling, "This you call fresh fish! They smell all over the place! They look half dead. And for this you are asking a schilling?" The poor farmer didn't know what to do. He could not let everyone in the market hear it, so he agreed to the ridiculous price that my aunt offered.

The next stop was a vegetable stand. My aunt touched and squeezed as many tomatoes as she could behind the farmer's back. And then she walked away to a fruit stand, where she would taste, and make me taste, every fruit on the stand. Then she made a sour face, saying, "The fruits don't taste good. They are sour." Then she started bargaining with the farmer until he got fed up with her and let her have the fruit for a cheaper price. My aunt did not stop there. She went back to the vegetable stand, where she picked all the tomatoes that she squeezed a while ago and said to the farmer, "How much are you going to charge me for these damaged tomatoes?" The farmer could not understand where the damaged tomatoes came from, but he could not argue. They looked damaged. So my aunt got them for a minimal price.

The funniest thing happened when we came to a dairy stand. In Europe, the butter did not come packaged. It came in cups or just bars. First my aunt tasted the butter and thought that it was a little bitter, so she bargained the price down. But then came another problem. She only wanted half of the bar, and the farmer would only sell the whole thing. My aunt had to find a partner for the other half of the butter. When she found one, my aunt insisted that she would be the one to divide the bar of butter, and she did. She did not divide it evenly. One half was bigger than the other. Wanting to show what a sport she was, she said to her partner, "Take any half of butter you want. I will take this." And then grabbed the bigger piece. That was my Aunt *Fiegelle the Koyekh*.

Vacation Days

AT THE END OF June, the school doors closed for the last time, to be opened again in September. The most desirable time of the year, the children's vacation time, was here. The children of Gusztyn welcomed it with open arms and expectations of having great fun. Our plans did not include camp, travelling, or going to the shore or the mountains. We were hardly aware that these things existed, so we did not miss them.

We spent our vacation walking around barefoot, in a slip and panties that also served as a bathing suit. We had no pool, not even a creek with running water, just a pond with muddy water and a lot of frogs. But nothing could keep us from bathing in the pond when the heat reached over one hundred degrees. Many times I would come home covered with mud and a frog on my back or in my panties. My sister would dump me in a barrel of rainwater to clean me up. When it did not rain for a long time, the pond dried out and the only place we could cool off was in a cellar, and that was where we spent most of the time.

We had other fun times. When the weather was nice, we went to the woods and picked mushrooms and chased rabbits and other small animals. But the best game was running through the fields, playing hide-and-seek. When we got tired, we would pick a cool spot under a tree and have a picnic with the food each of us had brought along. Usually it was two slices of homemade rye bread, some fruit, and some milk. When it was time to go home, we would pick wild flowers to make bouquets to bring to our mothers. Picking the flowers the first time made me very sad. Who was I going to bring flowers to? I had no mother. Even as a child, I was a very private person. I would not say anything to the other children. I decided that my older sister, Roza, who took care of me, was my mother. I remember that I handed her the flowers, saying, "You are like my mother."

Roza cried. Then she took me in her arms and hugged and kissed me, repeating, "You are my baby. I love you. You are my baby."

As I grew older, the things that seemed to be so much fun in the past did not appeal to me anymore. Since we had no radio, no movies, not even a Victrola, I became interested in reading. At first, I read children's stories, then novels, and finally, as the years passed, classics by Polish and Russian authors. The problem was that I did not fully understand all I was reading and I had no one to share it with, as the peasant children did not read.

One day, I got lucky. A Jewish family with a son, David, who was four years older than me, moved to our village. David was the only Jewish boy close to my age who I knew. I got to like him a lot. I think I had a crush on him, which I did not realize at the time. David seemed to be fond of me too. We spent most of the vacation time together, taking long walks, talking about what we read. He would explain things to me, which I did not understand. We went riding in his father's horse and buggy, and on Saturdays we went berry picking on the outskirts of the village.

One time, while hunting for berries, we noticed a large berry at the bottom of some thick bushes. As we both bent down to try to get it, David's arm went around me, touching my breasts, which had just started to develop. I shrank away but I got a sensation that I had never experienced before. Just a touch of his hand gave me such great pleasure. We were two youngsters, twelve and sixteen years old, with all the feelings and desires of any normal teenagers, but we did not express them in the way they do today; we did not expose them for everyone to see. It was something private, something special and almost secret.

That was the best vacation I ever had.

The Prize

IT WAS MY FIRST date, which seemed very promising. The previous one was a real disaster. It never came to be. The boy who asked me out stood me up. He took my friend out instead. This time, things looked good. I was dressed up in a light blue dress and black patent leather shoes, and my hair was in two braids with blue bows at each end. As I was only fifteen, I did not wear any lipstick, and makeup was something unknown to me.

My date showed up on time. He wore a pair of three-quarter navy jeans with an elastic band at the bottom, a matching jacket, a white shirt with a red polka dot tie, and a cap. He took me to the school dance. I wasn't much of a dancer. The only dance I liked and was good at was the polka. We had some refreshments, and then the teacher in charge of the party announced that there would be a prize for the best dancer of each kind of dance. The music began, and we started to move. First there was a tango, and then the fox trot, a waltz, and finally my favorite, a polka.

I considered myself to be a polka expert, and I was hoping to win a prize. We were dancing away until there were only two couples left on the floor: me and my friend Suzie. She too was a very good dancer. As we danced, the kids around us were clapping and yelling out our names. It seemed to me that there were more calls for Molly than for Suzie. I was very excited, feeling sure that I was going to win. As I danced very fast in front of Suzie, suddenly I felt a pull on my dress and then heard a rip. When I stopped and turned around, I saw that my dress was ripped wide open. I was very embarrassed, and ran out of the room. As luck would have it, my dress had gotten caught in the fan Suzie was swinging in her hands as she danced across the room.

I don't know if it was an accident or a deliberate act on Suzie's part. Naturally, I was terribly upset as I did not win the prize; Suzie did.

Wander Vest

"MOTHER, WHAT ARE YOU staring at? Please, let's go. It's late. The children will be coming home soon," I heard my daughter calling me. But I didn't move. My eyes were fixed on a mannequin in a far corner of a clothing store. The mannequin was half naked. The only thing she wore was a knitted vest ... a vest made of light and dark brown squares, with beige trimming all around it. I figured it must have been a very old-fashioned vest since I'd never seen a similar one and I had lived in the United States for the last forty years. I could not take my eyes off the vest. My thoughts were racing in my head, going back to my childhood.

When I was eight years old, we were quite poor; even though we had food, clothing was scarce. When my oldest sister, Roza, was fourteen years old, she had a coat made by a tailor. It was a brown coat with a white rabbit collar. It was the talk of the village. After she wore it for two years, the coat looked worn and faded, but that was no problem. The coat was ripped and the hem was done over on the left side, and everybody said it looked even nicer than it was before. Then it became Helen's coat. Two more years passed, and my sister outgrew the coat. It got too short.

So then it was my turn to get the coat. But after Helen wore it for two years, it was mostly worn out. My older sister decided that it was still a shame to throw it out. She cut out some squares from the good parts of the coat, sewed them together, put in a new lining, added some cotton, and made me a vest. It was a vest of light and dark brown squares since some parts of the coat were more faded than others. It was trimmed with beige all around.

I wore the vest for a long time. It came in handy during the war since it had a lining. I was able to sew some pictures of my family into the cotton. I hardly ever took it off my back. When the war was over, the vest was completely worn out. I took out the pictures and saved what was left of the vest. It was like a family heirloom handed down from one generation to another.

March to a Different Drummer

A LITTLE GIRL WITH blue eyes and blond pigtails, with a red ribbon tied on the top of her head—that was me, Malka Feuerstein. When we moved from Gusztyn, to Skala, I was very excited since the village school had only four grades, and the one in Skala had seven. I loved school, and learning came easily to me. My ambition was to become a doctor, to heal sick people, to prevent them from dying, as my parents did.

I made many new friends. Everyday, I would help them with their homework. Sometimes I wondered if it was my personality or their need for my help that drew them to me. When I finished the seventh grade, most of my friends, who were very rich, started talking about entering gymnasia or a university. It was then that I realized that all my ambitions and aspirations were nothing more than fantasies and empty dreams. Gymnasia and universities were out of reach for a poor Jewish child. I felt like all the doors were closing on me. There was nowhere to run. I felt lost and unhappy. All I had left was hope and a belief in G-d.

Then, one day, just like a miracle, everything changed. The Russians invaded the eastern part of Poland where we lived. I was thrilled, because at that time the Soviets did not discriminate. They judged you by your merits, not by your race, color, or religion. Now I could go back to school and achieve my dream. I was so grateful for the lucky break they gave me that I enrolled in a Communist Youth Party, called Komosomol. I broke away from all my old rich friends and joined a group of proletariats. There, I became acquainted with a group of poor young people with a very idealistic outlook and great conviction. We discussed and analyzed the teachings of Marx, Lenin, and Stalin, and dreamed of a beautiful free world for everybody. My family did not approve of my involvement with the Communists. In the first place, we were religious. Then they pointed out the terrible actions of the Soviet secret police, (The Peoples Commissariat for Internal Affairs) and the unjust rulings of the Communist party. They explained to me that whereas Socialism and Communism are beautiful ideals in theory, the Soviets turned them into a corrupt, deceiving monster. I became very disillusioned and hurt. My beautiful young dreams, my illusions, changed into a world of confusion. All I had left was my school. Even that was not meant to be for long. Soon, Hitler came and put an end to my work, my freedom, and my hopes. Not being able to continue with my education was one of the greatest disappointments of my life.

Fire

LIKE A WAVE OF black clouds before a storm, anti-Semitism spread over the villages and shtetlach of Poland in the early thirties. It swelled like a mild gale, mostly in the villages, where the peasants broke some windows in a Jewish stand, wrote anti-Semitic graffiti on houses, and distributed leaflets filled with hate and threats against Jews. In no time, threats became actions.

We read in the Jewish newspaper stories of a woman being killed in a nearby village, or about a Jew who was caught walking alone on the road being beaten and having his beard cut off with a knife while onlookers yelled, "Dirty Jew, go to Palestine." We all were very disturbed and worried. I remember going to bed each night, afraid to fall asleep, anticipating that something terrible might happen.

One hot summer night, as I was twisting and turning in bed, unable to fall asleep, I heard the loud ringing of the church bells. We did not have any fire engines in our village, so the ringing of the bells in the middle of the night meant that there was a fire. We all rushed outside. At first we saw a yellow pillar of smoke rising high above the houses and trees, and then, like a volcano, a burst of flame spread in all directions. We knew what it was: large bales of hay were burning on the grounds of an estate owned by a Jew. As there were no fire engines, the water had to be taken from a nearby lake, with people forming a line and passing buckets of water until the fire was under control. It took a long time. Most of the buildings were burned to the ground. Luckily, nobody was hurt except for some chickens and two little calves.

The morning after the fire, several empty kerosene bottles were found over the piles of ashes. Everyone knew it was arson. To top it off, a horse and buggy filled with some village hoodlums went around stopping at each Jewish house, throwing leaflets that read, "Dirty Jew, leave the village. Next time it won't be just chickens and calves. It will be you."

It was then that my family decided to move to a shtetl. The same anti-Semitism was there, but it was easier to bear it with many other Jewish people around. We suffered until 1939, when the Soviets invaded eastern Poland and freed us from the terror.

CHAPTER THREE

The War Years

(1939–1945)

The End of the Skala Jewish Community

ON SEPTEMBER 1, 1939, the Germans invaded Western Poland. A little over two weeks later, on September 17, 1939, the Red Army crossed the Zbrucz River, and from then until then end of June 1941, Skala was under Soviet rule. On June 22, 1941, the Nazis invaded eastern Poland. Then on July 8, 1941, Skala was taken over by the Hungarian Army, who were Nazi allies. By the end of July 1942, the German military controlled the area.

During the war, the cruelty and sadism of the Nazi high command could not be underestimated. In keeping with this brutal approach—what better time to surprise, humiliate, and disgrace their Jewish enemies than plan for some especially violent activity on one of the Jewish holidays.

With this in mind, my mother's family and fellow Jews of Poland knew to look out for "something special" during the High Holiday season of 1942. Sadly, they were not disappointed.

The *action* (death deportation) began at 6 AM on the first day of Sukkot, Saturday September 26, and ended at noon on Sunday, September 27, 1942. They started a pogrom that, by its end on Sunday, resulted in the capture or killing of almost seven hundred Jews. My mother and her siblings hid in a bunker built under the house. All but the oldest sister, Roza, made it into hiding in time. What exactly happened to Roza once she was captured is uncertain, but she was either killed and buried in a mass grave in Skala, or was one of the many women, elderly, and children who were selected to go to the death camp in Belzec. Less than two weeks later, an order was issued that by October 22, 1942, the surviving Jews of Ozieran, Mielnica, Korolowka, and Skala had to leave their homes and move to the central ghetto in Borszczow.

As Nazi oppression surged forward and tensions continued to build, on December 12, 1942, my mother Malka (Molly), knowing her fate was doomed if she stayed where she was, took a chance and left without proper papers, and boarded a train to an unfamiliar city, Zlochow.

Thou Shall Not Question G-d's Actions

I WAS BORN IN Poland, a tiny six-pound girl with blue eyes and blond hair. My three brothers had black eyes and black curly hair. In the first years of my life, I was treated like something special. But after my father died and my mother got ill, the rest of my family had no patience for me. I was too young to understand it. I attributed it to my looks.

I was different. I looked like a *shikse* (a non-Jewish girl). Why? I was Jewish. The problem was that the peasants' children laughed at me, calling me "dirty Jew," and the Jews called me "shikse." The older I got, the harder it was to adjust. I felt like I didn't belong, neither a *Jew* nor a *goy* (a non-Jew). But it wasn't until I became a teenager that I started asking questions. "Why don't I look like other people? Why do some stay away from me? Whose fault is it?" As usual, we ask questions but find no answers.

Then Hitler came. He showed me the reason why G-d created my looks. I survived the Holocaust, as my different appearance helped me hide my true identity of being Jewish.

Love

LOVE HAS MANY FACES and many definitions: admiration, devotion, tenderness, and affection.

When I was a teenager, I was very interested in novels that told about two people and their undying love. At that time, I read a poem by a famous Polish poet, Adam Mickiewicz. He wrote about himself and a beautiful girl, who were madly in love. On his birthday, his sweetheart sent him a rose; so did his closest friend and his mother. After a few days, the friend's rose died; a day later, the sweetheart's died too. Only his mother's rose remained fresh. Only a mother's love is true.

I became a bit confused since I had no mother. Did it mean I would never experience true love? It wasn't until the Holocaust that my belief in any kind of love was shattered. I saw a man who swore that he would kill himself if his sweetheart wouldn't marry him. They got married and had six children, whom he adored as much as his wife. However when the Gestapo knocked on the door, he left his wife and his children, and ran away to save his own life. I saw a mother leaving her twin one-and-one-half-year-old babies to be killed, hiding herself from the Nazis. People acted like animals with instincts, not emotions or reason, and the instinct of survival was the strongest one.

There was only one incident that I cannot forget or interpret. There was the first pogrom in our shtetl. Most of the Jews were gathered in one place to be killed or taken to the concentration camp. The only Jews who were spared were the ones who worked for the Gestapo, and the rabbi of our shtetl.

Fifteen minutes before the train was to leave, the rabbi put on his *tallis* and joined the other Jews on their way to the death camp.

Today versus Yesterday

THE DINING ROOM TABLE was set with an elegant Madeira tablecloth, crystal glasses, silver flatware, and fine, expensive china. The beautiful candelabra, with candles burning bright, and the crystal chandelier shone. The centerpiece of red roses made the table fit for a king. It was Rosh Hashanah night in my daughter Evelyn's house. We celebrated the beginning of a new year. The whole house was filled with joy and happiness. You could feel the spirit of the great holiday. You could say the *shkhine*, which means "divine presence," was spread in every corner of the room. As we all sat around the table, enjoying a wonderful dinner of traditional Jewish dishes, such as chicken soup with kreplach, kugel, tzimmes, gefilte fish, and other old-fashioned delicacies, I was overwhelmed with happiness.

As the night went on, my feelings suddenly changed. My mind started to wander far back, remembering another Rosh Hashanah night. In a small shtetl in Poland, I saw a small room with a dim light. The table was covered with a heavy, homemade piece of cloth, with clay dishes and tin flatware. Two brass candlesticks with unlit candles seemed to stand in the corner of the table, insulted for not being lit. The atmosphere in the room was depressing. We were afraid to light the candles so as not to arouse the Germans' suspicions. My family of three brothers and two sisters were sitting around the table in semi-darkness, eating our New Year's supper, which consisted of potatoes, bread, and water. We all had the feeling that something was going to happen.

The Nazis always planned something special for a Jewish holiday. It happened: before the night was over, they started a pogrom. We all ran to a hiding place: a bunker built under the house. Five of us reached the bunker and survived, but my oldest sister Roza never made it. The Nazis caught her, and I never saw her again. As if done by a knife, a stabbing pain went through me.

I snapped out of my nightmare and back to reality, which was so beautiful and safe. There I was, sitting with my wonderful family, surrounded by warmth and love. I have so much to be thankful for, and I am. But from time to time, I still go through the agony of the past.

Comment: The holiday was actually Sukkot, not Rosh Hashanah.
At six a.m. on Saturday, September 26, 1942, the first day of Sukkot, the Gestapo rounded up half of the Jewish inhabitants of Skala, including refugees from

neighboring villages. Those who survived this "action" (i.e. death deportation) were marched to the railway station and crowded into freight cars, seventy-five to eighty in a car. The selection later took place at the Janowska Camp in Lvov. Women, children and the elderly were sent to Belzec. The men who remained in the Janowska Camp were forced to do heavy labor. Those who stumbled or fell behind were killed. As noted earlier the details of Roza's death are unknown.

Mazel - מזל

IT'S A SMALL WORD, so often used in everyday life to express a fortunate happening, a positive experience. The interpretation of the word מזל (or mazel) is simply "luck." I personally feel that מזל is somehow different from just luck. It has a deeper, a stronger meaning.

I had a lot of mazel in my life that could be easily explained as a series of coincidences. There is only one experience in my life that I consider pure mazel.

It was the beginning of the Holocaust. At that time, I was staying with my Aunt Sara and her daughter, Lisa. One day we got the terrible news that there was going to be a pogrom. My aunt decided that we should all run away and hide in the nearby woods. We hardly had any clothes. It was a dark and cold December day with a slight drizzle. My aunt found two old scarves and put them over her and Lisa's heads. She had no scarf for me, so she took a small crocheted afghan with big holes, folded it into a triangle, put it on my head, and tied it like a babushka under my chin.

I very much resented wearing an afghan on my head. My aunt comforted me, saying, "It is true, it does not look too good, but you will see. It will be *mazeldik* (full of luck)."

We came to the woods and hid under some bushes. We stayed there for a long time without making a sound, afraid to breathe. Suddenly, Lisa sneezed.

At that moment, as if from nowhere, we heard footsteps. I looked up and saw two Gestapo men coming toward us. We started to run, each in a different direction to confuse the Germans. I ran for a long time with the Gestapo close behind me. I was running between very thick bushes, and it was very dark, so he could not see me. Maybe that is why he did not shoot me. Suddenly I felt a pull under my chin. The Gestapo caught the afghan on my head. He was pulling it in all directions. I realized that his fingers must have gotten tangled up in the holes of the afghan. At that moment, an idea struck my mind. I untied the knot under my chin and left the afghan tangled up in the hands of the Gestapo. I ran away, losing him. The afghan that I resented wearing so much brought me mazel. It saved my life. I never saw my aunt or my cousin again.

A Chanukah Miracle

CHANUKAH, THE HOLIDAY OF Lights, is a time of joy, gratification, and festival celebrations. It is the time for latkes and jelly doughnuts. For me, Chanukah, latkes, and jelly doughnuts have a special meaning. It was during World War II when Poland was occupied by the Nazis. It was in the year 1942, when the Gestapo started the process of making the cities and towns *Judenfrei*, which means "free of Jews." They would gather a large group of people and just kill them or load them into cattle trains and send them to concentration camps.

After one such pogrom, in which I lost some of my family, I felt that I must do something. I couldn't just wait there to be killed. I was a seventeen-year-old girl, blond with blue eyes and a very light complexion. I looked like a typical non-Jewish Polish girl. So I decided to go to a faraway city where nobody would know me and no one would know that I was Jewish.

But it was easier said than done. Because I lived in a small village all my life, which I had never left before, just going on a train for the first time was a big endeavor for me, aside from the great danger the trip represented. To make sure no one was Jewish, the Germans were checking everyone's passport or other documents. For a big sum of money, you could get an Aryan passport, but I was very poor and couldn't obtain one. I decided to go anyway. I knew I had nothing to lose; I would die either way.

It was December 12, the first day of Chanukah. My sister packed a bundle with some clothes and some food for me to take on the way. I took off my yellow Jewish star, which every Jew was forced to wear on his right arm, and I went to the train station. I bought a ticket, walked into the last car, and sat in the far corner, frightened to death.

All of a sudden, I heard some commotion at the door. I looked up and saw a Gestapo officer coming into the car. He was checking everybody's bundles and documents. I suddenly realized that the food that my sister had packed was a deadly weapon that would surely kill me. She had packed Chanukah latkes and jelly doughnuts: traditional, symbolic Jewish foods. I knew then that even if by some miracle I could talk my way out of not having a Gentile document by lying—saying that I'd lost it or forgotten it at home—I could never explain the latkes and doughnuts in my bundle.

What happened in the next few minutes I can only describe as some kind of miracle. As I sat there paralyzed by fear, not able to move or even think clearly, I saw the Gestapo officer coming toward me. At that moment, a little girl who was sitting next to me with her mother, eating an apple, suddenly stood up and ran across the car, spitting out the apple all over the floor. The Gestapo officer took one more step toward me, slipped on a piece of the apple, and fell. I don't know what happened to him. I was too stunned, too flabbergasted to ask questions. I saw some people carry him out of the car, and then the train pulled out of the station, taking me to my destination.

I realized then that Someone up there wanted me to survive.

*This story, "A Chanukah Miracle," was originally a short story printed in The Jewish Woman Magazine in December 2008 on Chabad.org and is now printed here with their kind permission.

Destination

DESTINATION, IN MY CASE, was hardly more than a word. All it meant was that I survived the trip and got off the train alive. But where was I going? To whom should I turn? What was my destination?

I stood at the train station, confused, my thoughts in complete chaos. In front of me stood a very big and strange city, Zlochow. I was upset and frightened. I knew that I couldn't stay at the station any longer without drawing attention and suspicion. Then I remembered hearing that there were newspapers in the big cities with want ads.

So I bought a newspaper and started looking for a job. Since I had no skill or experience in any field, I decided to take a domestic position.

I was hired by a Polish couple as a maid. They didn't know that I was Jewish. They asked me all kinds of questions. Where did I come from? Why did I leave my home? Who were my parents? Although I had been orphaned since I was three years old, I lied again, saying that my parents were involved in the Polish underground. I explained that they were sought by the Germans so I had to run away from home. Then came the questions that I expected. The question of the times: "Are there still any Jews in your town?" the man asked, "because here," he said, "we just kill them and make soap from their remains."

That was my formal greeting, and that's how I became, Mary the maid.

Being a maid in Poland was the lowest position that someone could get. You were not considered a person. You were a nobody. Being dehumanized was bad enough, but making the transition from Molly Feuerstein to Mary Weisniewska was the hardest thing I had ever done. I had to watch every word I said, every move I made. I was afraid to fall asleep at night, fearful that I might talk in Yiddish in my sleep.

During the daytime, I was terrified whenever I saw a German coming my way. My whole life was a nightmare. I felt like a person who has been sentenced to death, just awaiting the executioner.

But the most horrible thing happened the day of a pogrom. That day I had to go to the store to buy some food. As I was leaving, my employer said to me, "Mary, while you go to the store, you should look and see how the Germans kill the Jews. It may come in handy." I felt like dying at that moment. But I had to go. What kind of excuse could I give without making her suspicious? So out I went.

What I saw could only be described as hell on earth. It left an impression in my mind that can never be erased. I saw big trucks full of naked, half-dead people—adults and children, screaming and pleading for mercy. I saw the Germans and their accomplices chasing the Jews through the streets, gunning them down in cold blood while others were laughing and making fun of it all.

I ran from the scene like a wild animal, not knowing or even caring where I was going. Inside, I was torn to pieces. My pain was unbearable. I ran for a very long time, until I was out of breath and had to stop. I knew I had to get back home so I would not make them suspicious.

When I got home, I just laid down, claiming a bad headache. I felt no physical pain; even the mental pain seemed to subside. I felt completely numb—no emotions, just an empty feeling inside me, a total deadness. But I didn't die. We had a saying in those days: "You don't die unless they shoot you."

A New Neighbor

ONE MORNING, I WAS awakened by my employer. "Mary, Mary," she called. "I have something important to tell you." She seemed very nervous.

I ran down, anticipating that something bad had or was going to happen. "What is wrong?" I asked.

"I don't know," she said. "But last night, Sue, our neighbor, came over and said that every morning she sees a large dog sniffing around our house. You know what that means, don't you? He smells a Jew."

My heart skipped a beat but I forced myself to smile and said, "What does that have to do with us? We have no Jews here."

That entire day, I walked around in a daze, frightened to death, expecting any minute to see the dog with a Gestapo, looking for me. I was relieved when the day was over, but the night was not any better. I had nightmares.

The next day, I got up early in the morning, looking for the dog. Sure enough, there he was: a beautiful, big, white and black dog. I had been told that the Germans used such dogs to smell out Jews. For a few days, I walked around like a zombie. Seeing the dog each morning, running around our house sniffing, I could not take it anymore. My boss kept on asking me, "What is wrong with you, Mary? You seem to be absentminded."

I decided to get rid of the dog. I bought a bottle of iodine, mixed it with a piece of chopped meat, and watched as the dog came, ate it, and ran away. I did not see him for a few days so I figured he must be dead. I was so relieved.

A week later, however, the neighbor, Sue, came to visit us again. "Eva," I heard her saying to my employer. "You remember Mr. and Mrs. Pollik from around the corner? They have no children, just a beautiful dog named Baby. A few weeks ago, Mr. Pollik died. The dog got very sad and hardly ate. He just crawled around the neighborhood. One day he returned home, very sick. Mrs. Pollik called the vet, but the dog could not be saved. He died the same day. The vet said he was poisoned with iodine."

I froze on the spot, realizing that I had killed an innocent enemy. This was the meanest thing I ever did in my whole life.

Almost Done

ONE DAY I WOKE up with an unpleasant feeling, waiting for something terrible to happen.

My lady employer was in a very bad mood too. Nothing I did pleased her. I was happy when she left for work. I did my usual chores: I fed the cow and the pig, I cleaned the house, and I gave the baby a bath and put her to sleep. As it was a very cold day and I saw that the brick oven was almost all burned out; to prevent the heat from escaping, I closed the chimney. After an hour, I tried to wake up the baby, but seeing that she was sleeping so peacefully, I let her sleep. When she did not wake up after another two hours, I got frightened. I picked her up and she felt like a dead body. I kissed her. I shook her. I slapped her. Nothing worked. She would not wake up. I was panic-stricken. I suddenly realized that the baby might have died from carbon monoxide poisoning. I closed the chimney too soon. I may have killed the baby. First I opened the chimney. Then took the baby outside. I was lucky the baby started to breathe and then cry. I cried hysterically, repeating, "G-d, take me away. I can't take it anymore."

When the day was over, I was completely drained. I just wanted to die. I lay down to sleep. I experienced something unusual. I was half asleep and half awake. It was a lethargic sleep. Suddenly, I saw a shadow of my dead sister, Roza, blowing into the room. She touched me with her very cold fingers and then said, "Do not despair. You see there is a tall mountain in front of you that keeps you in the darkness. You must keep climbing until you reach the peak. There you will find sunshine and freedom. G-d will be with you all the way." With these words, she left the room. At that moment, I woke up or just returned to reality. I didn't know then and still don't know if I fell asleep and had a dream, or daydreamed, or if my mind gave way and I hallucinated. I was in shock, unable to think clearly or rationally. My body was stiff with fear. But I did understand the message of the apparition: I had to continue to fight. I must go ahead until I reached the peak, the freedom. I knew that I would overcome all of the obstacles, all of the horrors of the Hitler hell.

It was then I knew: I would survive.

When I returned home to my shtetl after the war, I discovered another horrific event had happened the same day as my dreamlike experience: my warm, loving, brother Mendel was killed by the Nazis. He was stabbed in the heart and cruelly left to die.

The Golden Bracelet

It was Christmastime in 1943. In Poland, as in most other countries, Christmas was celebrated on a very large scale, with parties and exchanging of gifts.

This being my second Christmas in the house of my gentile employers, I learned how to prepare all kinds of holiday dishes and how to decorate the tree and sing Christmas carols. The people for whom I worked were very pleased with my work as a maid. While they did not pay me much for my labors, they did want to show me their appreciation. They decided to give me something really special for the holidays.

My employer took me to a jeweler and told me to pick any sample of bracelet that I liked and the jeweler would make it up for me. I picked something very simple but beautiful. While showing the jeweler the bracelet I had picked out, I saw him take a small bundle out of the safe and spill its contents on the table in front of me. I took one look at the display and felt my whole body stiffen from shock. On the table I saw about twenty gold teeth. I did not have time to guess where all these teeth came from because the jeweler was very anxious to tell me the details.

"You see, Mary, all these teeth," he said, "they were pulled out of the mouths of living Jews, not by a dentist but by us. You should have seen their faces and heard their screams when we pulled their teeth with pliers and strings. I will make you a beautiful bracelet from them."

How can I describe my feelings at that moment? I knew that I must accept the bracelet so as not to make anyone around me suspicious. Every time I put it on my wrist, I felt like thousands of nails were digging into my flesh. It was terrible torture. I could not get rid of this bracelet of misery until the day I was asked to give it back. That was the day that my employer found out that I was Jewish.

The Pig

"BUBBE. BUBBE. COME HERE!" I heard a cry for help as I walked out into the garden behind my daughter Evelyn's house. It was my four-year-old granddaughter, Elysia, buried in a bed of golden leaves, trying desperately to get up but slipping back every time she made an effort to stand up. I rushed to her rescue. While pulling Elysia out from under the pile, the feel of wet leaves on my hands and the rustling sound of the leaves under my feet triggered a disturbance in me—a feeling of longing for something or someone. I felt like going back somewhere but did not know where or why.

Before I had time to analyze and rationalize my strange feelings, I got the answer from the most unexpected source.

The telephone rang in the house. As I picked up the receiver, I heard my daughter Rosalie's voice. "Mommy, are you and Daddy busy today? If not, maybe you would like to join us? Soly, Ryan, and I are going to an animal farm."

"We'd love to go," I said.

"Fine, we will pick you up in half an hour."

At first, as we came to the farm, I was disappointed. There were very few animals. But my three-and-a-half-year-old grandson, Ryan, had a great time chasing the chickens, ducks, and geese. As we walked deeper into the woods, we saw some goats, sheep, rabbits, and finally a pigsty with two big pigs and a few little ones. One of the larger pigs was a natural color with a black patch on top of his head. Seeing this animal brought back some memories. Suddenly I recalled another pig that looked exactly like this one.

It was during the Holocaust. The people I worked for as a non-Jewish maid had this pig hidden in a bunker so the Germans could not find him and take him away. The bunker was a little, square, boxlike room without doors or windows. The only opening was in the ceiling, through which we fed the pig.

One time my employer found out that the Germans were going to catch some non-Jewish girls and boys to send them to work in factories in Germany. My employer suggested that I hide in the pigsty.

At first I was very upset staying with the pig. I don't know who was more scared, the pig or me. After a while, I calmed down and tried to talk to him, telling him that the two of us were in the same predicament. "If the Germans find either of us, we will be killed, so please let's be friends." For a while, the pig just stared at me, and then he started approaching me. I was petrified. I had nowhere to go, nowhere to hide. I moved to a dark corner, where I laid down on the bed of leaves, which I had prepared for the pig a few days ago. I hoped he would not see me, but the leaves were wet and slippery, making a rustling noise under my feet. The pig came closer and closer to me. He touched me with his snout and smelled me all over. He oinked a few times, and then lay down next to me and fell asleep. I was shivering from cold and fear, but realizing that he would not hurt me, I pressed against his warm body and relaxed. I spent two days and two nights with the pig, sharing his bed and the food that was thrown down to us.

When I came out of the pigsty, I developed a strong attachment to the pig. I was very concerned, knowing that the plan was that he was to be killed for Christmas. I knew that I could not prevent it. The only thing I could do to show my loyalty to him was refuse to eat his meat, which I did.

Please Don't Forget

IT WAS SPRINGTIME. IN Poland, spring was the most beautiful time of year that one could ever imagine, but for me it holds the most horrible and painful memories.

Spring was the time when the Nazis were at their most brutal and performed their most inhumane acts. It seemed as if the beauty of nature only brought out the beast in them.

On one such Sunday morning, I was walking the streets, pretending that I was in church so that the people I worked for as a maid would not find out that I was Jewish. The weather was just beautiful. The trees and the flowers were blooming. The birds were singing, and the air was filled with the sweet smell of spring. Everything around me seemed so quiet and peaceful.

However, I was not at peace with myself. I felt as if I were being torn apart. The beautiful spring morning awoke very mixed emotions in me. On the one hand, there I was, a young girl, partly free—at least walking in the sun, full of life, dreams, and desires of a normal teenager. On the other hand, I felt very guilty—guilty for being alive, for my dreams, for my desires. I felt like a traitor. How dare I have these feelings while my brothers, my sisters, my people, were being murdered in cold blood.

As I was walking, I saw a man and a woman coming out of an alley. Behind them was a German Gestapo pointing his gun at them. I knew that they were Jewish. I was sure they knew as well as I did where the Gestapo was taking them: to the graves at the outskirts of town. There, he would either kill them immediately or throw them into the graves half alive and allow them to bleed to death.

As I walked close behind them, I heard them speaking in Yiddish, saying, "How can we tell the world what is being done to us? How would anyone believe it?"

As I passed by them, the woman started speaking in Polish, directing it to me without turning toward me. "Little girl," she said, "we are going to be killed, and may be buried alive. Please don't forget what I am telling you and what you see happening here. Please remember it and tell others not to forget."

I am sure she did not know that I was Jewish. All she saw was a little girl. Although I was eighteen, I looked no more than twelve. I was thin and undernourished. I am sure she hoped her words would leave an impression on the innocent young child. And they did!

I was frightened that the Gestapo might get suspicious of me, so I did not respond in any way. I just walked by them and continued down the street. But the woman was right. I will remember it forever. And I must tell it over and over again so that the world will never forget!

Friendly Advice

GIVING ADVICE IS SOMETHING we all like to do at one time or another. A little advice in everyday life is normal and accepted. Giving advice on important issues could be very serious and sometimes even harmful. While a particular bit of advice is good for one individual, the same advice is not necessarily right for another with the same problem. Though our intentions might be well-meant, we are not always in control of what happens next.

I was very lucky in receiving the right advice. During the Holocaust, I was advised by a family friend to leave my hometown in order to save my life. It was the best advice I ever received. Being very grateful, I wanted to do the same for someone else. I wanted to save somebody's life. I had a very good friend, Clara. She was blond with blue eyes. She could very easily pass for an Aryan too. I advised her to come to Zlochow, the city where I was. She came, and I found her a job. For a while, everything was going smoothly. After half a year had passed, Clara was discovered by the Gestapo and was taken away. I was sure she was killed. I felt very guilty, blaming myself for Clara's death. If I had not given her advice, she might have survived in some other way.

It was not until after the war that I found out that Clara had survived after all. As it happened, Clara was a very pretty girl. When the Gestapo brought her in to be killed, a Polish policeman asked the Gestapo to let him do the killing. The Gestapo agreed. The policeman took her out, and instead of killing her, he took her home. He fell in love with her and saved her life.

I felt very lucky about the outcome since the advice that almost destroyed a human life saved it after all.

Decisions

How ARE WE TO know which turn to make? Which path will take us on the right road of life? Are we rulers of our own free will or makers of our own choices? Or is it just destiny?

As a teenager, I had many choices, many important decisions to make, while pretending to be a non-Jewish maid. One day the ground caved in under me. I stood paralyzed, in total shock, not able to move. I had just been told by my employers that they found out that I was a Jew. They were nice about it; they did not turn me over to the Gestapo. They just asked me to leave their house.

It was a nasty, foggy day. I had nowhere to go, nowhere to return to. Thoughts of suicide came to my mind. I realized that I could not do this for two reasons: First, I was very religious, and second, I did not have the courage. Contemplating my situation, I felt I had no other choice but to give myself up to the Gestapo.

With a bundle under my arm, I walked the streets for hours, going nowhere. Then I came to a hill on the outskirts of the town, in a place I had never been before. I don't know what brought me there. It started to rain. The sidewalks, covered with leaves, became very slippery. Suddenly, something caught my attention. I noticed an old woman in a wheelchair. It seemed she had lost control of the chair and was sliding down the hill. I ran over and tried to stop it, but I could not do it myself. I held on to it, dragging along, slowing it down. I screamed for help. Some people came over and helped me stop it. The old woman was in shock. When she came to, she invited me to her home. Seeing the bundle under my arm, she asked me where I was going. When I told her that I had just been fired from my job, she said, "I cannot help you because I am poor. However, I have a rich sister who lives in another town. She could use some help."

The next day, I was on my way to Lemberg. Her sister did hire me, and I liked the job. I felt safe there. Only one thing bothered me. My employer's husband had a mistress, who was his wife's best friend. The two lovers would behave in a very inappropriate manner, paying no attention to me, as if I did not exist. For some reason, the other woman, whose name was Helen, pretended to like me. Once, through the slip of the tongue, I told her that I had a sister who was in danger of being killed by the Nazis. Helen wanted me to leave my job and come to work for her, promising to bring my sister to me.

I refused her help. I did not trust her, knowing she betrayed her best friend. I thought perhaps she just wanted to hurt her friend more by taking me away from her. More important, I could not be so ungrateful to the old lady who had jeopardized her sister's life for me. If the Germans ever found out that she was helping a Jew, they would kill both of us.

At last, the war was over. I survived physically, but mentally I was left a cripple, full of guilt, regrets, and bitterness. Even now, many years later, I still wake up in the middle of the night in a cold sweat, tormented by the thought that maybe I should have taken Helen's offer. If only I had listened to her, maybe, just maybe, my sister would be alive today. I argue with myself. My logic tells me that I was right, that probably we both would have been killed. But my conscience does not ignore all my worries, and I cry myself to sleep … only to wake up the next morning knowing that I can never bury my past and that there will be other nights when the ifs, the onlys, and the maybes will return.

In the Bunker
A Monologue

I REMEMBER HOW HAPPY I was swimming around in the warmth inside of your body. I was never cold or hungry. From time to time, you would pat me with your loving hand, telling me you loved me and how you couldn't wait for the time when I would come out into the world. You promised me a world full of sunshine and love, where everybody would welcome me with open arms, eager to hold, hug, and kiss me.

Mother, what went wrong? I was born, but not into a world of sunshine or loving arms. Instead, you put me into a dark hole deep under the ground, with strange people who frighten me rather than love me. When I cry, they all come around me and yell at you, making you cry. Why are you crying, Mother?

Are you frightened too? You're picking me up and holding me tight, close to your heart. It feels so good, but I cannot stop crying. I am hungry and my stomach hurts.

Mother, why are you putting me down? I want to be close to you. Oh, I see you; are taking a pillow, putting it on top of me, trying to keep me warm. But, Mother, why are you covering my face with it and pressing hard on it? I can hardly breathe. I am suffocating. Mother, please don't do it. I don't want to die. I am so tiny, so innocent. But I understand. They made you do it.

Good-bye, Mother. I love you, and I forgive you.

Mommy, Tell Me Why

The winter is over
There's spring in the sky
You hear the birds singing
You see children play

    Some people are walking
    With bright, happy smiles
    They are full of life
    Full of hopes and desires

But there are other people
Who live deep underground
In cold and in darkness
From the murderers, they hide

    These are our people
    Who try to survive
    In greed and in hunger
    Fighting for their lives

You see there, a mother
With a child by her side
She's trying to save her
To preserve her life

    She sits in the bunker
    In darkness of night
    With her little girl
    Clinging to her tight

The child is only five
She can't understand
Why she must sit still
She can't make a sound
Why is she confined
To this hole in the ground?

She must not talk loud
She can't laugh or cry
So she's asking a question
"Mommy, tell me why?"

"Why can't I go out
And play in the sun?
You said winter is over
All the snow is gone.

"Spring has come, you said
With sunshine and flowers
With birds in the sky
I hear children playing
Mommy, why can't I?"

So she sits in the bunker
Trying not to cry
While her child keeps asking
"Mommy, tell me why?"

It's a pretty story
But the truth is sad
The angel she will meet
Is the angel of death

She promised her heavens
Angels in the sky
But how could she tell her
That she's going to die?

Chapter Four

The War Is Over

(1945–1949)

The Aftermath

RETURNING TO SKALA AFTER the war, Malka learned the devastating toll that the years of violence had exacted on her home. Of the prewar population of two thousand Jews, only one hundred and fifty had survived. Although Malka knew that her sister Roza was a victim of the first *action*, she was devastated by the news of the deaths of her three brothers, Rubin, Mendel, and Leib, and her sister Helen. Not only was she an orphan, but now she was truly alone, without any living family. On February 3, 1945, she married another Skala survivor, Sam Greenberg, a man ten years her senior. He too had lost whatever family had lived in Skala prior to the war—both of his parents and his younger sister, Hannah. Together, like many other homeless European Jews, they travelled from Poland until they were able to find some security in a displaced persons camp, called Fohrenwald, in Germany.

The Mezuzah

IN 1941, THE GERMANS invaded the eastern part of Poland, where I lived with my family. This part of Poland had been occupied by the Russians since 1939. The news about the German troops moving toward our town was very disturbing and confusing to all of us. Some people were telling us about the horrible actions of the Germans against the Jews, while others were saying that they didn't believe it. They thought that the people of a nation that supposedly was very advanced and highly intelligent could not turn into such brutal, barbarous murderers.

I remember my own sister, Roza, saying, "The people of Heine and Goethe could not do any such things." Very soon, she and all others found out how very wrong they were. Our village Skala, was on the Polish -Russian border, so we could have escaped to Russia before the Germans came. At first, we decided to do so. We packed some of our belongings and valuables to take along on our journey, and we hid some in the basement. We took a few bricks from under the steps, put the valuables in the opening, and then cemented the bricks back into place. In there we also hid all of the mezuzahs that we had taken off the doorposts; we didn't want them to be destroyed by the Germans.

We did not escape. We were caught by the Germans. At first, the Germans limited their actions to taking the money, gold, and other valuables from the Jews and just occasionally killing a few of them. After a while, they started the pogroms. It was then that I left our town and went far away.

After the war, I returned to my hometown. I did not find any members of my family. My three brothers and two sisters were all dead, killed by the Germans, and so were most of the Jews of my town. From two thousand people, only one hundred and fifty were left alive. I went back to the house where I had lived before the war. I knocked on the door. A Gentile man came out, and, recognizing me, he refused to let me into the house. I told him that I just wanted to go down into the basement to see if maybe I could find some of my family's belongings. He laughed in my face and said, "Go ahead—look." When I went down into the basement, I saw that the bricks under the steps had been removed. The hole was empty, and everything was gone. The only thing that I found in the far corner was one mezuzah. I guess they did not see it because all the others were torn to pieces. The parchment was scattered all over the basement. In one of the corners, I also found the remains of my sister's half-rotted raincoat. I took the mezuzah and what remained of the raincoat and left my old home forever. I could never go back there.

I cleaned the remnant of the raincoat and saved it. I will cherish it all my life. As for the mezuzah, it became my lucky charm—a family heirloom. I have carried it with me through all the journeys of my life. It is the only heirloom from my very traditional Jewish home, a reminder of my childhood, of a life and a past that is no longer there.

A Tear, One Tear

THIS IS A POEM that was originally written by my mother in Yiddish in 1944. She had it translated into English

The storms are over
The nightmares are gone
No whistling of bullets
No echoes of bombs

No more howling of dogs
Which filled us with fear
No sounds of the sirens
That meant death was near

You hear no more crying
Of babies in pain
Nor pleading for mercy
Of mothers in vain

You hear no more shouting
Of German SS
Who shuffled the bodies
Into chambers of gas

The war is over
(Suddenly it's quiet)

The chimneys stopped smoking
The air's clear of smell
Of burning bodies
That were trapped in hell

The earth soaked with blood
Of innocent people
Is trying to dry
In the hot rays of the sun

She tries to shake off
The most heavy burden
The greatest injustice
That was to her done

The war it is over
The tyrant is gone
The world was set free
A new era begun

The nations emerged
From a dreadful ordeal
To build a new future
With freedom and justice
Without violence or fear

A lone man arises
From the depths of despair
From the most horrible tortures
That a human could bear

With eyes open wide
He looks all around
So as to make sure
That he is alive

He looks at the flowers
The birds and the trees
They all seem to whisper
"You survived; you are living.
You are free, you are free."

He walks with brisk steps
Toward a brighter tomorrow
Trying to forget
The grief and the sorrow
But something minute
In the human body
Will remain forever
As it was before

Untouched
By the freedom
By the spring or by sunshine
And laughter it knows not at all

What is the phenomenon?
Everyone was asking
That is not being moved
By a thing in the world

Is it a thing
Of strength and of power?
Or is it a thing
Of unusual might?

It is not a thing of unusual power
It is not a creature
That has any strength

In the eye of an orphan
Is one tear—congealed
One that remains there
When by millions they fell

The tear's a reminder
A symbol eternal
An everlasting trace
Of the Hitler hell!

Love Letter

"No documents of any kind. No letters. No books. Nothing written in Polish." That was the order given to us by the leaders of the Bricha, the organization that took care of the Jewish survivors of the Holocaust. We were passing the Polish border on our way to Germany, disguised as Greek Jews. Poland did not want to let the Jews go. It was very ironic: they did not want us there, yet they would not let us leave. They wanted to show the world their tolerance.

I was very upset because I had some letters from my family and a letter from my first boyfriend, Fabian. It was my first love letter. It was very short. I was very young, and he was much older. He wrote, "Dear Malka, I don't know whether I should write to you as a child. You are too old for that, but you are too young for a woman. I can only write that I miss you, and all I want is that we both survive and see each other again. Waiting for you. Love, Fabian."

I hid all the letters from my family in the lining of my coat. Fabian's letter I put into the foot of the boot that I was wearing. When crossing the border, the guards checked everyone, looking for money or jewelry. They stripped everyone. As I got undressed, I was told to take off my boots. The guard searched all my pockets, and then she put her hand into the boot, and she found the letter. To her, it must have seemed like just a piece of paper and she was not interested in it. She was looking for money or jewelry. She tore up the letter and threw it away. It was then that my first love letter became just a memory.

The Secret

It was April of 1944, the beginning of the end of Hitler's regime. The Russian army was moving closer and closer. Lemberg, the city where I was hiding out as a non-Jewish maid, was bombed daily by the Russians and the Americans. We could always distinguish the difference between the bombings: the American raids came mostly in the daytime. They were very precise and accurate in their targets: airports, railroads, and military facilities. The Russian raids were very chaotic and unorganized. They just threw the bombs in any direction. One time, we were awakened by an air raid siren. Since we had no shelter, we were told that the best place to be was in the open. The other maid and I ran to the garden. It was a spectacular nightmare. The sky was lit up from thousands of anti-aircraft bullets. The bombs made a whistling sound as they fell and loud explosions when they touched the ground. On the far horizon, we saw a big ball of fire slowly coming down to earth. Suddenly, it got quiet. The raid was over. The following morning, we read in the newspaper that a Russian plane was shot down and one pilot was missing.

The next day, I crawled into a bunker to get some potatoes. Suddenly, I came face-to-face with a man. His clothes were torn and dirty, and he smelled of smoke. His face was unshaven and filthy. He looked very frightened. I knew immediately that he was the missing pilot. He asked me not to tell anyone that he was there. "All I want," he said, "is a drink of water and a piece of bread." I gave him a glass of milk and some bread. I knew I had to tell my employers about him. I was sure they would not betray him since they were very anti-German. I was right; they viewed it as a big privilege to rescue an enemy of the Germans. That night, he was taken to a nearby house that had stood empty for years. He hid out in the attic. Only one thing puzzled everyone. He refused to be examined by a doctor, even though he was assured by my employers that the doctor was a very reliable man. The pilot claimed that he came from a certain Russian sect that did not believe in medicine.

Since I was the only one of the servants that knew about him, I would bring him his food daily. He told me his name was Greenspan. Every time I came, he asked me to stay with him for a while. He spoke to me about the great Russian writers—Tolstoy, Dostoevsky, and Pushkin—and their works, most of which I had read. One time when I was about to leave, he took my hand and said, "Mary, I want to tell you something, but it is strictly confidential. You have to swear that you will not tell it to anybody." I agreed, not realizing what was coming. "My name," he said, "is Hershel Cagandovich. I am a Jew. I have a wife, Natasha, and a daughter, Sonia. She is about your age. They live in Babince."

I stood there, as if struck by lightning. I could not move or talk. I had only one thought, Why in the world did he choose me to tell the truth to? He could not know that I was Jewish. I spoke perfect Russian. I looked like a real shikse who had just left the farm, and I thought I acted like one. Why did he have to burden me with his secret? I had enough problems hiding my own identity. He had no right to do it to me. Right or wrong, he did it, and I gave him my word. Now I was responsible for his life. Now I realized the true reason why he refused to be examined by a doctor.

Four months later, the Russians liberated Lemberg. Hershel was free and ready to go back to his military service. Before he left, he took me aside and said, "Mary, I knew the entire time that you were Jewish. There were three things that betrayed you. First, you knew too much for a little shikse who came from a small village; second, when you get excited, you talk with your hands; and third, whenever I asked you about your family, the answers were very inconsistent. You would close up and your eyes would get that faraway look, so full of pain that only a Jew could recognize."

He handed me a piece of paper with the name and address of his wife. He told me that in case I did not find anyone from my family, I should go to her, where I would find a home. Three months later, I returned to my shtetl, Skala. There were no survivors from my family. I was left all alone. I just wanted to die. But you don't die just because you want to; life goes on.

In time, I met my husband, and when we were about to get married, I received a letter from Hershel's wife. "Dear Malke," she wrote, "I am sorry to let you know that Hershel is not with us anymore. He got killed while flying over Berlin. But before he died, he wrote me about you and asked me to welcome you as my daughter. My home is open for you, and my Sonia will be happy to have you for a sister."

I was deeply touched by the letter. I wrote to Natasha, telling her how grateful I was for her most generous offer and explained why I could not accept it. A few weeks later, I got married, and we left our shtetl to go to an uncertain destination.

I never heard from Natasha again.

I Love You Not for Your Virtues but in Spite of Your Faults

I WAS SITTING BY the hospital bed, holding my friend's hand. Memories of my youth came flashing through my mind like slides in front of my eyes.

There we were, two youngsters: me and my best friend, Millie, whom I loved very much. Millie was very pretty, tall and slim, with long blond hair, blue eyes, and a beautiful nose. We were inseparable. We did everything and went everywhere together. We always promised ourselves that we would love each other and be friends forever.

When Millie got to be fifteen years old, I noticed a change in her. She would not spend as much time with me as before. She became interested in men. What disturbed me was that she always got involved with older men. One time she came to me and told me that she was going to a big city to stay with some friends. When she came back after a few months, her beautiful blond hair was changed to red, and her face was covered with a lot of makeup. It was the first time that I saw changed hair color and a face so painted, as we called it then.

It frightened me. I realized that she changed drastically, that there was something wrong, but when I asked her, she denied it. She said that she felt great and she had a wonderful time. People were whispering about her, but young girls were not allowed to listen.

My family asked me not to be friends with Millie. But I loved her too much to give her up, so I saw her from time to time, secretly.

Then the war broke out. We were separated. I left my village in order to save my life. And Millie, who was not Jewish, remained at home. When I returned home after the war, I tried to find Millie. I had been told that she was no good. She became a drunk and a crook. She had fallen to the lowest level. She became a prostitute.

A short while later, I was told that she was very sick. I tried to find her and I did, in a state hospital, dying. When I looked at her lying so pale and quiet, I felt very sorry for her, and, in spite of all the bad things I had been told about her, I still loved her very much.

Mayn Scheichlech (My Shoes)

IT WAS AUGUST 1945. The war had just ended. The survivors from the concentration camps from all over Europe were trying to get back to their countries. The Polish Jews wanted to leave Poland, hoping to emigrate to the United States or Palestine. Although they didn't really want us, the Poles made our leaving difficult. As we arrived by train to the Polish/Czech border, we were searched, robbed, and interrogated. As I was standing in line, waiting for my turn to be called, I felt someone pulling at my arm. I turned and saw a woman holding a little box. She handed it to me and said, "Please, miss, hold this for me. Don't let go of it. But don't open it. I will tell you all about it after I come out of the interrogation."

I took the box and held it. When my turn came to be interrogated, I gave the box to my friend, Lucy, who stood next to me. "Make sure you don't lose it, and when your turn comes to go, hand it to the person next to you." The interrogation was over, and the little box survived by being passed on from one another. As the woman who owned the box returned, she grasped it and raised it to her heart. We introduced ourselves. Her name was Regina Rosenfeld. "Molly," she said, "I promised to tell you the story of my precious box. I was born and raised in Poland," she began. "I was a very lucky person, born to a wealthy family, married to a wonderful man, and I gave birth to a baby boy, Mendele. My life was like a fairy tale, but not for long.

"In 1939, when the Germans invaded Poland, all of my world shattered … it fell apart. At first, my husband was taken away into the Polish army; then my family was sent to a concentration camp. I remained with my younger sister, Susi, and my little three-year-old baby, Mendele. We were hiding in an attic. One time, while I was in another room, I heard the attic door open. I saw through the keyhole two Gestapo. They ordered my sister to take the baby and come with them." Suddenly, Regina stopped talking. She started to scream, "I did it! I let him die!" She became hysterical. After a while, she calmed down and continued her story. "You see, Molly, I saw my baby being taken away to be killed and I did not run to him. I could not move. I stood as if paralyzed. Then, I heard my baby's voice, 'Aunt Susi, I cannot go. I need mayn scheichlech.' Susi reached under the bed and gave Mendele the shoes, but the Gestapo grabbed them from his little hands and threw them away. I could still hear my baby's cry as the Gestapo threw them across the attic. 'I want mayn scheichlech. I want mayn scheichlech.'

"After they left, I went to the attic and found the little shoes on the floor. I put them in a box and buried them under the attic floor. All I wanted was to die. We were taken to a concentration camp, but I survived. I came back to the attic and found the box with the scheichlech. I will never let them leave my hands again. Maybe Mendele will come back. I know he is dead, but maybe he will come." She started talking irrationally.

Another victim of Hitler's hell.

The Wedding

WALKING DOWN THE AISLE was Sara, the beautiful bride, in her gown of white lace, a long veil, and a head cover made of flowers. She looked like a dream. She walked slowly with a radiant face and her black eyes sparkling with happiness. She was about to marry Moses, the man who was waiting for her at the other end of the aisle.

The bride was a survivor of the Holocaust. Most of the guests in the temple were friends and well-wishers. Everybody was joyful and feeling happy for Sara and Moses. The temple was completely still; everybody's eyes were fixed on the lovely bride as she moved graciously, step by step, toward the chupah.

"Stop her! Stop her!" Suddenly, came the outrageous screams of a man standing in the doorway. Everybody's head turned toward the door. "She cannot get married. She is mine!" The bride turned around. She took one look at the stranger and then let out a hysterical cry and fainted. The stranger kneeled next to her, trying to revive her, repeating constantly, "Saralah, Saralah, it is me, your husband, Louie." When Sara came to, we heard a very sad story, but not unusual for the time.

Sara and Louie were living in a bunker as man and wife for two years. One night Louie went out to get some food and never came back. Sara was heartbroken. She was sure that he was killed. After surviving the war, Sara met Moses. They fell in love and decided to get married.

Louie was not killed. He was caught by the Gestapo and sent to a concentration camp, where, by some miracle, he survived. When he returned home, he started looking for Sara. Finally he found her when she was about to marry another man. The wedding was stopped.

After a few weeks, Sara realized that the relationship that she had with Louie was not a real marriage. They were two young people stranded together in a small hole by fate, by circumstances rather than love. She decided to marry Moses, the man she loved.

Laughter

I GREW UP IN a house filled with laughter, even though we had no parents and we were rather poor. Somehow we managed to be happy and carefree. Our house was always full of fun. My friends loved to come to my house and play. They felt free there, with no restrictions from older people. My oldest brother would sit with us and tell us stories or teach us games. I always walked around with a smile.

As time passed, things started to change. Hitler came into power and sent his deadly armies all over Europe, and eventually they reached our shtetl. However, it was not until the actual invasion by the Nazis that we felt the impact of it all. The laughter turned to anguish and grief. The smile on my face faded away. Later, after I left my home to save my life, the smile was replaced by a grimace that resembled a smile, but the real smile was gone.

Returning home after the war and learning about my entire family's death, I thought that all my smiles and laughter had died forever. But, as they say in Yiddish, "*Man tracht un Got lacht* (Man plans and G-d laughs)." Something happened that was so insignificant and even childish that it proved me wrong: I found a friend, a survivor. We were born and spent our childhood together in a small village. I called him my cousin although we were not related. When he saw how lonely and unhappy I was, he got a little white dog to cheer me up. I called him Sniezik, which in English means "Snowy." I walked with him for miles and sometimes even talked to him when I felt very lonely. When winter came with cold and deep snow, I had a problem. I could not get a coat for Sniezik, so I crocheted one for him, plus four booties for his legs. I remember the first time I put the coat and the booties on him and took him out for a walk. I put him down in the snow, but he could not stand; the booties were in his way. Slowly, he got up, trying to walk. He picked up one leg and put it back, then another one and put it back again. He did it with all four legs but did not budge an inch. Then he tried to go backward, repeating the same routine. Watching him was the funniest thing. I burst out laughing, a free, uncontrollable, real laughter. I laughed so hard that tears came to my eyes. Then I started crying hysterically. I realized that the laughter in me had not died.

I felt that the wounds of my crippled soul and mind would mend. I could still find some peace within me. It was then I realized that there could still be some laughter left in my life.

Charity

In Gusztyn most of of the peasants living there were poor and existed on the sale of the crops they raised in their fields. The three Jewish families were just as poor. One had a grocery store, which was robbed every now and then by the village hoodlums. The second was a tailor, who did not make enough money to feed his family of eight children. The third was our family of six orphans. Our oldest brother ran a small tavern, hardly making a living. In spite of the poverty in the village, we had no beggars because the peasants did not beg; they just stole. The Jewish beggars who came from the nearby shtetlech were helped by their fellow Jews. My family never refused a needy person, even if it was only a groschen or two.

One time, as I was playing with some peasant children, a young man came over to us and asked if someone would show him where a Jewish family lived. Without telling him that I was Jewish, I took him to our house. As he walked, he stretched out his hand, which meant that he wanted charity, and then he said, pointing at me, "This shiksele brought me to you." (While my brothers and sisters had black, curly hair and brown eyes, I was born with blonde hair and blue eyes. It appears that G-d creates us to be set for our destinies.)

"This shiksele," my brother said, "is Malkele, our youngest sister."

The young man just said, "I am Srulek. Can I sit down?" As my sister Roza explained to me later, he seemed as if he was going to faint. She gave him a glass of milk and some bread, which he swallowed in a few seconds.

Then he told us he was a tutor; he had no money and nowhere to go. His parents had been killed by a train when their horse got frightened and ran onto the train tracks. We could not keep him, but my sister took out a steak that we had hidden and gave it to him. When Srulek left, my brother argued with Roza. "How could you give away a steak? It is half of the food for the children for a week."

"We will get by somehow," Roza answered. Then, turning to us, she said, "Remember, children, that when someone stretches out his hand, don't ever let him go away empty. Charity is the biggest mitzvah a Jew can give."

We never heard from Srulek again. The war came, and the war was over. I was the only survivor from my family. I got married and went to a DP camp in Germany.

While standing in line waiting to be assigned a room and some food certificates, I felt that someone was staring at me. I looked up and saw a man looking at me and smiling. Then he came over to me and said, "How are you, shiksele?" I still did not know who he was. I figured out that it must be someone who knew that I passed as a shikse during the war. "Shiksele Malkele, don't you recognize me? I am Srulek. Where is your sister, Roza?"

Then I realized who he was. "I am the only one alive. All my family was killed."

His face changed and his eyes filled with tears. We cried together. "Your sister Roza was a real saint. I knew that when she gave me the steak she deprived herself and you children of some food, but she saved my life. I have never forgotten her."

He then told us that he was appointed to be in charge of the DP camp. He took us out of the line and gave us a decent room and some food.

A Gift

I WAS AWAKENED IN the middle of the night by a pain that felt like the blade of a knife ripping through my body. I was half asleep and did not know if I was having a nightmare or if the pain was real since it disappeared before I was fully awake. It left me shaking and frightened, and it was an hour before I finally dozed off again, only to be awakened by another pain, more severe and lasting much longer.

At that time, we lived in a displaced persons camp, Fohrenwald in Germany, where there was a little hospital but no ambulance. I knew I had to get to the hospital, but I was unable to walk. My husband held me around my waist and literally dragged me to the hospital. When we reached our destination, only one doctor was on duty. He examined me and told me that everything was all right and that I should go home. "No, doctor," I said, "I am staying here until all the pain is gone." That was about five o'clock in the morning. I stayed in the hospital all day, walking around when the pain was gone and lying down in the bed, crying and complaining, when the pain got severe.

My poor husband was with me all day, not eating, wringing his hands, and praying, "Please, G-d, let it be me. Give me the pain."

By five o'clock that afternoon, I was completely drained. Suddenly another pain came that was so severe that I passed out. When I came to, I saw the doctor standing by my bedside, my husband crying, and a nurse with a little bundle in her arms. "Molly," she said, "look. Here is your baby girl." She put the baby in my arms, and I saw my daughter. I touched her sweet face and her little hands. I burst out crying. It was a cry of happiness, the greatest joy I'd ever had. It was not only because I had a baby, but also because this baby represented so much more to me. She was part of me—she gave me a family, the only family I had in the world. We named her Jochewet after my husband's mother. She was a beautiful baby and grew up to be a wonderful human being.

A Tear—II

(composed after the war in 1944 and later translated into English)

A Tear, a Trace of Hell

The storm has already passed.
The sun shines anew.
The blue heavens reveal themselves again.
The earth breathes easily and freely.
The springtime of humanity has yet arrived.
Freed are the nations from the yolk.
The sun of freedom spreads its rays,
It awakens, it arouses the heart from the slave.
Ripping the chains, the person comes back to life again
To build, to create anew.
The face becomes cheerful, the heart becomes light.
The spirit is raised and free.
Only something, a tiny thing in a human being
Remains unable to be raised
This is not a soulful being
That has in it power.
This is a frozen tear
In an eye without shimmer or light,
The soul that cannot be moved and cannot
Be aroused by anything.
In the world, this is a trace of
Hell.

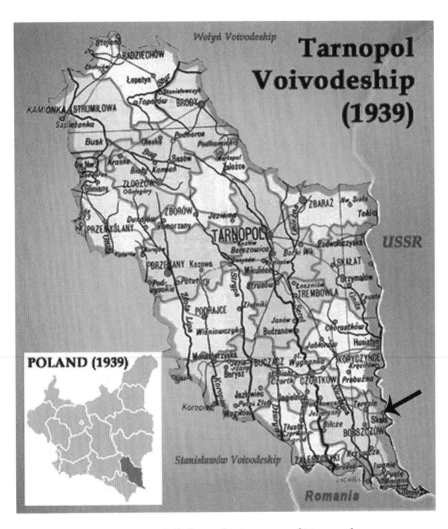

Location of Skala in the Province of Tarnopol
1939

Elka, Rubin, Roza, Mendel, Malka (Molly), and Lieb 1939

Malka's School Photo 1930's

Molly and friend   *Molly as a teenage girl in Skala*

Skala Street

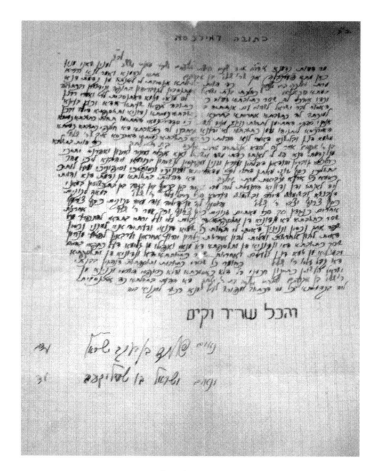

Married February 3, 1945
Marriage Contract

Sam (center) with friends at DP camp

Sam and Molly

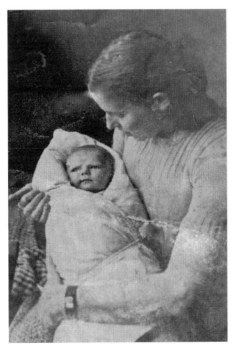

Molly and Evelyn 1946

Sam, Molly and Evelyn in DP Camp

CHAPTER FIVE

America

(1949–1995)

The Trip to America

So WITH PROPER PAPERWORK in hand, my father and mother, their two-year-old daughter, and many of their fellow displaced persons left Germany on January 10, 1949, on the *Marine Marlin*. The ship, launched in 1945, was built to carry thirty-eight hundred troops and a crew of two hundred and fifty-six. As it was a military ship lent by the United States to assist in bringing émigrés from a post-war Europe to America, it was not in any sense a luxury passenger vessel. Though grateful to leave the destroyed former homeland, those taking the nine-to-ten-day voyage across the Atlantic Ocean to start a new life found the journey difficult. Many of the immigrants were overcome by seasickness for much of the voyage and could barely get around the boat. I remember my mother saying how horrible the trip was for her and so many others on the ship. She would tell the story with pride about how her little Evelyn, just a toddler, acted as a caretaker, running up and down the ship, bringing water to those in need, i.e. those who were too seasick to get it on their own. To my mother, this was an example of my sister's inner strength. Her Evelyn was not a victim. She was a caretaker and a survivor.

Relief occurred ten days later on January 20. Molly always spoke of her joy at coming into New York Harbor and seeing the Statue of Liberty, which she fondly called *the Lady*. Although Ellis Island was the gateway to a new life for many immigrants, the *Marine Marlin* continued past *the Lady* and travelled up the Hudson River until it reached its destination: Pier 57 on Manhattan's West Side (long since torn down). For some unknown reason, the press was at the port when the incoming immigrants arrived, and my sister, Evelyn, had her photo taken and printed the next day in one of the local New York City daily papers.

How proud my parents must have been.

The Hospitable Lady

IN 1945, THE WAR was over. People were travelling all over the world. Some were coming home from prisoner-of-war camps, some from battlefields, some from hiding, and others were coming from the death institutions of the concentration camps. I returned home to Skala. It was then I learned my brothers and sisters were all killed by the Nazis and their accomplices. I was exhausted physically and mentally, I felt crushed, totally destroyed.

In my grief and sorrow, I was very lucky to find a wonderful man who in time became my husband. Since my husband had a large family in the United States, we decided to emigrate there. Although I knew I had to go, it was very hard to leave my hometown forever, the place where I was born, where I spent my childhood with my loving family—the streets where I played with my friends. The most painful thing was leaving behind the lonely graves of my parents, knowing that I would never see or visit them again. I felt that I had betrayed them.

Our journey to America was a long and very hard one. We had to cross the borders of Poland, Hungary, Austria, and finally, Germany illegally. In Germany, we were put into a DP camp, a camp for displaced persons. Our lives in the DP camp were very difficult. Four families lived in one small room, without enough food or clothing. Children born there were often undernourished and sick. It was under these circumstances that my oldest daughter, Evelyn, was born. No matter how hard life in the DP camp was, to us who had survived the Holocaust, it seemed like paradise. After living there almost four years, we received our visas to go to the United States.

We travelled on an old warship named *Marine Marlin*. The first day of our journey was a very happy one. We were leaving behind all our grief and sorrow. We were on our way to a new, great country, where we hoped to find a new, happy life.

When I woke up the next morning, I felt I was going to die. I was seasick, and so was my husband. The only one who was all right was our two-year-old daughter, Evelyn. I got very upset. The thought that after surviving the Holocaust, I might die on the ship, leaving my baby and my husband alone, petrified me. I remember praying, "Dear G-d, make me live in a basement on bread and water, but let me get to the shore." We travelled for nine days. On the night of the ninth day, we came close to the shores of New York Harbor. It was then that someone yelled out, "Look, there she is!"

We all came on deck, and that is when I saw her for the first time, standing so tall and so proud with the burning torch, like a gracious queen. With her arms outstretched, she seemed to embrace us, to welcome us to her great country. The Statue of Liberty—the symbol of freedom!

I cannot describe our feelings of joy and ecstasy. It seemed as if she touched us with a magic wand and revived us. Suddenly we all recovered from the seasickness. Some people were singing, and some were laughing. Others were crying hysterically. Everyone was overwhelmed with joy, happiness, and new expectations.

I will forever remember and cherish that moment. It marked for me the beginning of a new and happy life in the golden land of America.

An Unfinished Story

As told to me by Mary and Sol Goldberg from Lemberg

THE TINY KEROSENE LAMP threw dark shadows across the small, dingy room, making it even dimmer. David and Susan and their two-year-old son, Benny, were sitting at the dinner table. No one touched the food in front of them, though on the surface, everything seemed to be normal. The minds of Susan and David were racing. They had to make a life-or-death decision. They had learned that there would be a pogrom in a few days. They resigned themselves to meet what Fate had in store for their future, but what about the baby? They considered two options: taking him along but risking his life, or leaving him with their Aryan maid, Mary, who promised to take care of him and hide him from the Nazis. Susan and David knew that they could not fully trust Mary since she was very anti-Semitic. They picked what they thought was the lesser of the two evils. In the middle of the night, they wrapped their baby in a blanket and brought him to Mary. As Susan told me later, leaving Benny felt as if someone was cutting her heart out.

The pogrom came as expected. The couple was taken away to a concentration camp, where David died in the gas chamber. Susan survived. Upon returning to her hometown, she went looking for Mary and Benny, but there was no trace of them. She asked around, going from village to village, but nobody knew or they would not tell her their whereabouts. All her efforts were in vain. Someone told her that there had been heavy battles in their town when the Germans were retreating and many people had perished. Susan resigned herself to the idea that Mary and Benny must have been among those who died.

After a few months, Susan left her hometown and ended up in a DP camp in Germany. In time, she remarried and had another child, a baby boy, which eased her pain, and her broken heart started to heal.

In 1947, Susan and her family decided to immigrate to the United States. While waiting to go through customs in New York, Susan suddenly saw Mary on the other side of customs, talking to a woman while holding a little boy. Susan thought she recognized him. It was her Benny! She ran through customs, calling, "Benny, my baby!" The little boy did not even turn his head, as he had probably never heard this name before. However, Mary recognized Susan. She grabbed the little boy and ran out with the other woman, got into a car, and sped away. There was no way of tracing them since there was no one listed on the passenger list under the name of Mary Kopeck and son.

All broken up, with her wounds wide open once again, Susan's life became a living hell, an endless search, an unfinished task.

If

IF ... A SIMPLE TWO-LETTER word. But how very important and significant it is in our lives. Often I wonder what would have happened to me if I had not taken that train from my village to the big city. Would I have survived? Would I be alive today? Hundreds of horrible pictures come into my mind. I see myself in a ghetto living with ten people in one room in filth and starvation, waiting to die or to be killed. Or perhaps I would have been sent to a concentration camp, where I would have been starving and possibly been beaten to death. Or I could have faced inevitable suffocation in a gas chamber with so many of my people.

But if ... I had not taken the boat to the United States after the war, I would have missed the great experiences I had here. Living here in this free country gave me a wealth of opportunities. I raised a family in a manner that I could never have done in Europe. I am so thankful.

What's in a Name?

Coming to the United States was the luckiest break I got in my entire life, although the beginning was very hard. Aside from the fact that my husband made a very poor living, I was very lonely. I had no family, no friends. So every Saturday, my husband and I went to the HIAS (Hebrew Immigrant Aid Society), where we met people who had just come from Europe, people like us. One time I met a friend of mine who came to the United States in 1939. He was married. His wife's name was Chancie. I knew him by the name of Dovid. I was so happy to see him. I hugged him and kissed him, repeating, "Dovid, Dovid, is it really you?"

"My name is not Dovid," he said.

"What do you mean not Dovid? What is it, David?"

"Nisht (not) Dovid and nisht David. My name is Nisn."

"Nisn, why Nisn?"

"Well, when I came here, everybody who talked to me would say 'Nisn, how are you? Nisn, come here. Nisn, go there. Nisn, do this. Nisn, do that.' I tried to tell them that my name is not Nisn, it's Dovid, but nobody listened to me. So I decided that maybe they are right. In English, Dovid must be Nisn. So I changed my name to Nisn. Soon after, I found out that they did not say Nisn. When they talked, they were saying, 'Listen,' but to me it sounded like Nisn. But it was too late. My name was changed. From then on, I would ask the other person to write down any word that I did not understand."

"You want to hear something even funnier?" Nisn said. "One time my uncle took me to a shoe store so I could buy a pair of shoes. The shoes had to cost five dollars and forty cents. I gave the storekeeper two five dollar bills. He gave me back five dollars and said, 'Maybe you have the change; give it to me.' I did not understand the word change. My uncle wrote it down for me. C-h-a-n-g-e. In Polish, Change reads as Chancie. 'What you want I should give you my wife Chancie for a pair of shoes!' I yelled and ran out of the store, leaving my uncle embarrassed."

"Now I know how funny it was, because now I speak perfect English." Nisn laughed.

New Experiences

WHEN WE CAME FROM a German DP camp in 1949 to live in the United States, the abundance of food and the luxuries of life were overwhelming. But the biggest thrill I got was when we were invited for a weekend visit to our rich Uncle Moe's.

To me, his house looked like a palace from a page of a fairy tale book. But that was not all. After a gourmet dinner, our uncle took us to a special room that he called a family room. It was there that I saw it for the first time. He called it a television. I was flabbergasted. Can you imagine? I thought, a talking movie in your own house! It was fascinating. Then and there I decided that as soon as we saved some money, I would buy a television. It took a while, but I got what I wanted: a Dumont television.

The shows were great. The Hit Parade on Saturday night, I Love Lucy, Kate Smith. There were children's show like Howdy Doody, Uncle Miltie, and Kookla, Fran, and Ollie. And at last came the commercials, the one for cigarettes, "Call for Phillip Morris," or the Texaco one with Milton Berle. But the one that stayed in my mind the most was the Hoffman Soda commercial. It went like this: "You don't have to go to a university to know what you should do when you are thirsty. Take Hoffman, drink Hoffman. Hoffman is the finest when you are thirsty." It was my three-and-a-half-year-old daughter Evelyn's favorite. Maybe it was because every time the commercial was on, I gave her a glass of soda instead of milk.

Next door to us lived an old, senile man. His name was Mr. Hoffman. One time when I came down with Evelyn, I saw the old man standing and mumbling something to himself. I stopped for a minute and said, "Hello, how are you, Mr. Hoffman?"

Before he could answer my little Evelyn started yelling, "Hoffman Soda, Hoffman Soda." The old man seemed annoyed. He just walked away without answering my greetings. It happened every time Evelyn saw the old man.

Finally he got very angry and told me to stop Evelyn from saying it. But how do you stop a three and a half year old from talking? One time she was playing in the backyard when I heard a scream. I rushed outside, and there was Evelyn, crying hysterically. "He hit me, he hit me!" she was sobbing and pointing to Mr. Hoffman, leaning against the wall.

I was outraged. "How could you do it?" I yelled.

"Nisht geferlekh (Not so terrible)," he said. "I did not hurt her. I gave her two hits on her tushe so maybe she'll learn."

I had it out with him, and he promised never to touch the child again. As for Evelyn, she was scared, but every time we passed him, she would grab my hand, hold it tight, and say under her breath, "Hoffman Soda, Hoffman Soda." This commercial became a family joke. From time to time when our family got together and someone asked for a soda, Evelyn would say, "You want a Hoffman Soda?"

From Primitive to Modern

LIFE IN OUR LITTLE village was very primitive. We had no electricity, no electrical or gas appliances. We heated our homes with wooden stoves. The cellar served as a cooler in summer and kept the vegetables, meats, and fruit fresh, and in winter it prevented food from freezing, rotting, and smelling.

It wasn't until after the war and coming to the United States that I discovered the wonders of electricity and gas. I was very impressed with my Frigidaire. My Aunt Fanny told me how to keep it clean and take care of it. "Molly," she said, "make sure you never leave cut fruit or uncovered food inside. It will smell up the Frigidaire."

During the first year, we were often invited by my husband's family for dinners and lunches. One time we were asked to my husband's cousin Bernie's, the doctor's, home.

First we were shown the house, which looked like a mansion. Then we were asked to sit down at the table for an appetizer. The kitchen was next to the dining room. When my cousin opened the Frigidaire to serve the appetizer, the fruit cocktail smell spread over the dining room table. We just looked at each other without saying a word. But Evelyn, my three-and-a-half-year-old daughter, asked, "Mommy, what smells?"

"No, Evelyn. Nothing smells."

"But It does smell over there. Ha ha, it smells!" she laughed. I was so embarrassed. I did not what know to say.

Luckily my cousin came to my rescue. "Molly, don't feel bad," she said. "Evelyn is only a baby. And it does happen that a lot of scents get mixed up and can combine to give off an unusual odor." She laughed, and everybody laughed with her.

1938 Sixty-Seventh Street

WHEN WE FIRST CAME to the United States, my husband, my two-and-a-half-year-old daughter, Evelyn, and I lived in a two-room apartment. Above us lived a man, alone. He was very unpleasant. He would knock around, move chairs, and make a lot of noise throwing things around the apartment and on the floor. But most disturbing was the fact that he would loudly listen to his record player until all hours of the night, waking up our baby time and again. We pleaded with him to not play music so loud, but all he would say was, "It is my home. I can do what I please. My home is my castle. I am the king."

A few months passed and there was a vacancy of three rooms, two floors up. We moved in and were very happy to get rid of our unpleasant neighbor. Now we lived on top of him. But we would not disturb him unnecessarily.

One time in the middle of the night, there was a knock on our door. It was our downstairs neighbor. "Look," he said, "how could you go to sleep when my ceiling is all wet, dripping straight on my head? You left your faucet open."

"I am sorry. My faucet is closed. Something must be broken. Why don't you call the super?"

He ran down and came back in a few minutes. "Look," he said, "the super is away on vacation. You did it on purpose to get even with me."

I got very annoyed. "I did not do anything, but even if I had, let me tell you something. This is my home. My home is my castle. And I am the queen. I can do whatever I please." I shut the door in his face and went to sleep.

Aunt Fanny, Mamele

YESTERDAY WAS THE YAHRZEIT of our Aunt Fanny. Since we had just come from Europe, we called her Tante Fanny. She was my husband's aunt, but I loved her dearly. My husband had a large family in the United States: a grandmother, four aunts, three uncles, and countless cousins. But Tante Fanny was my favorite. She was the only one who took us in, who received us with open arms. She was sweet and warm. She made us feel wanted.

She gave us her own bed while she herself slept on a made-up bed. She took care of my baby when I had to go somewhere. She made me feel like part of the family. Although she could not read or write, she had a lot of native intelligence and a heart of gold. She was a real mensch. Despite the fact that I loved her dearly, I hurt her, not deliberately or intentionally.

It happened a few years later. My husband went into business and became very successful. We bought a house with a big backyard. At that time, I had two children, ten and six years old. I bought them a portable pool. It was deep and long enough for a grown person to soak in. Aunt Fanny went to the beach every day since we lived only fifteen minutes from the ocean. When I got the pool, she would come to the pool every day before going to the beach. One time while in the pool, she made a remark.

"It's a pleasure," she said. "After I finish my housework, I don't have to take a shower before I go to the beach. I just come to the pool and wash myself." Her remark made me very angry.

Without thinking, I burst out, "Tante Fanny, you cannot go in dirty to the pool where my children are."

She did not say a word, but the painful expression on her face told me all. She was hurt deeply. She never came to the pool again. I felt terrible. The worst part was, she died within a few weeks. I understand that it had nothing to do with my hurting her, but nevertheless, a regret and feeling of guilt was left hanging over my head for a long time.

The Beach

My husband and I and our two-year-old daughter, Evelyn, came from Europe to the United States in January 1949. At the beginning, our life here in the new country was difficult. The hardest thing was not knowing the English language. My husband's aunt and uncle, with whom we lived for a while, could not write or read English; their spoken English was very poor too. As for traveling, they depended on following landmarks to get to where they were going. We got into the habit of doing things their way. In time, we moved into our own apartment. It was the beginning of the summer. I was told that we lived a short distance from the beach at Coney Island.

One day I decided to go to the beach with my baby. I did not know how to get there. I went to our Aunt Fanny for directions. "Take the train until you get to the end of the ride. Then, walk straight for a while until you see the sand and water." When everyone got off the train, we followed them to the beach. When it was time to go home, I became terrified. How would I be able to get back?

As I walked the platform, I saw a little stand with bagels, candy, and cigarettes. I got lucky. The woman in the stand was speaking Yiddish. She told me to take the Sea Beach train on the other side of the platform. "Don't worry," she said, "the train only goes in one direction." I realized then that my aunt did not tell me in which direction to go to return home. When I finally got back to our apartment, I was wet from head to toe … not from the ocean water, but from heat and anxiety!

Kolade

"MY G-D, LOOK AT all this food!" I overheard a young woman talking to someone I thought was her mother. They spoke in Russian. For one moment, a picture of myself flashed in front of my eyes. I saw myself in her place, saying the same exact words to my aunt forty-three years ago when we first came to the United States. We lived with my husband's aunt and uncle. They were treating us very nicely. Only one thing was missing. The food they gave us was very scarce. I guess it was sufficient for two old people, but for us, young and always hungry, one small boiled cutlet, one small baked potato, and two tablespoons of canned peas and carrots just wasn't enough. As time passed, my husband got a job as a butcher and brought home his first paycheck of $20.70. The aunt became my manager. She took $10 and put it in the bank in my name. The second ten she said I could spend on food and clothing.

The first time she took me and my daughter, Evelyn, shopping, we went to a store called Key Food Supermarket. When I walked in, I could not believe my eyes. Such an abundance of food! It took my breath away. "My G-d," I said to my aunt. "Look at all that food!" My aunt just smiled. I did not know where to look and what to take first. I wanted to buy everything I saw. But my manager was beside me making sure that I did not go overboard. "Remember the sum of money that you are holding has to last you all week." Though not too happy, I bought just the bare necessities.

In all the excitement, I forgot to watch my Evelyn. I looked for her, but she was nowhere to be seen. I knew she must be somewhere in the store. Finally, I found her in front of a candy and chocolate stand. "Mommy, mommy," she yelled, "kolade!" (In her language, it meant chocolate.) She stood there with her dress rolled up to her waistline, filled up with chocolate bars. I pleaded with her to put them back but she would not listen. I tried to take them away from her. She cried and screamed. People were stopping and talking to me. I did not understand a word they were saying since I did not speak English. Like G-d sent from heaven, a woman came over and spoke to me in Yiddish. She took my daughter and bought her the chocolate. I was so grateful for the gift, but most of all happy that I found a woman my age speaking Yiddish. We became close friends. As she used to say while introducing me to her family and friends, "This is my biggest bargain. For 80 cents, I bought myself a friend for life."

To Forgive but Not Forget

AFTER THE SECOND WORLD War, most of the Holocaust survivors came to the United States. My husband, our two-year-old daughter, Evelyn, and I were among the first ones to come. At the beginning, our lives were not easy, living in a strange land with a foreign language, though we were lucky. My husband's family was good to us. They took us into their home until my husband found a job and we could afford an apartment on our own. It was only one and a half rooms in a fourth-floor walk up. To me, who lived for years in a displaced persons camp, in one room with three other families, it looked like a palace. In general, the American people were nice to us—very friendly, very understanding. I had just one very unpleasant experience, which stayed in my mind for years.

One day my husband brought home his weekly paycheck. To cash it, I had to travel to the bank by bus, twenty-five blocks away. When I got on the bus with my little daughter, all I had was 12 cents. I paid 7 cents bus fare and was left with only 5 cents. I was not concerned about getting home. I knew that after I cashed the check at the bank, I would have enough money.

But as it happened, my husband forgot to sign the check. Naturally the bank would not cash it. There I was, 25 blocks away from home, with a baby in my arms, hardly speaking any English, and only 5 cents in my pocket. And my wardrobe wasn't up-to-date either. I did not know what to do. I was desperate. So when the bus came, I tried in my broken English to explain to the bus driver what had happened. But he would not listen. He just told me to get off. When I did not move, he simply pushed me off the bus. I was very hurt, very embarrassed, since there were other people on the bus. It was unbelievable, though, that nobody offered to give me 2 cents. I walked home for 25 blocks with the baby in my arms. When I got home, I became hysterical. Not only was I totally exhausted physically, I was about to collapse mentally. I could not take anymore. After all the abuse and humiliation I went through during the Holocaust, an experience like this just about destroyed me.

As time passed, my husband got a good-paying job. We decided to move to a bigger apartment. The minute I saw my new landlord, I got an unpleasant feeling that I knew him from somewhere. At first, I could not place him. After a while, I remembered. He was the bus driver who pushed me off the bus.

I knew it would be very unpleasant to see him every day. When I first approached him, he said he did not remember me. But sometime later, he admitted that he remembered the incident. He apologized, saying it was not his fault. "A lot of bums and beggars are trying to get a free ride," he explained, so it was his responsibility not to let them. I believed him and forgave him ... but I have not forgotten.

Why Do I Hurt?

Why do I hurt?

What are the feelings that tear me apart?
Why is the pain so deep in my heart?
Why is my soul tortured day and night?
What is the fear that holds me so tight?

Why do I hurt?

Is it the past that haunts me forever?
The cry of the millions who died in great pain
Or the sobs of a mother pleading for mercy
While watching her child being killed?

My heart bleeds for one and each soldier
Who was lost fighting for survival
Of our Holy Land,
Whose young life is threatened.

I am so confused
So full of despair.
What help can I give them?
I can't even cry.
My eyes have no tears.
They are cried out, dry.

Reserved

EVERY TIME I MET Chaim at HIAS (Hebrew International Aid Society), he would ask me the same question. "Moishe, so what's doing today? Did you think of something new to tell me about Yankele the *ganif (a thief)?*" He had been told that I was the only one who saw Yankele before his death. I knew what Chaim wanted to know. But he never asked me the right question.

"Chaim, sit down," I said, "and let me ask you something. What are you? Some kind of investigator? If you want to find out something about Yankele, why don't you just come to the point and ask me directly instead of going all around it? I know that you did not like your nephew, Yankele. Most people did not. But how many people knew him, including you? Why all of a sudden such concern? Where were you when your nephew and niece needed your help? If I remember right, you never wanted to have anything to do with them or your brother. You were ashamed of being related to them."

I remember Yankele as a healthy, beautiful little boy with black curly hair, big brown eyes, and a smile that warmed your heart. He was roaming the streets of our shtetl barefoot and ragged. His mother abandoned him when he was only five, and his sister, Rifka, was nine years old. Their father worked as a blacksmith. Very often, he would come home late at night, drunk, yelling and cursing. Many nights, the children went to bed hungry since their father would spend the little money he earned on whiskey for himself.

Being raised in the streets, Yankele soon learned how to survive. Yes, he became a ganif. But he was a very bright boy even though he never went to school. He taught himself to read and write, but he never stopped being a thief. "Remember, Chaim, that they used to call him a genius in his profession." He was a very pleasant, outgoing youngster.

The only person he did not get along with was his father. If you just mentioned his father's name to him, his usual laughing face would freeze and his eyes would get that hard, faraway look. His sister, Rifka, was a pale, thin girl, reserved, with a frightened look in her eyes. "Chaim, did you ever know it or care? No. You were ashamed."

Yankele was seventeen years old when the Germans invaded our shtetl. As soon as they started pogroms and sent Jews to the concentration camps, Yankele, with his family and ten other people, built a bunker in the woods, where they hid. Life in the bunker was very difficult, but the people were bearing it well, except for Rifka. She was getting thinner, paler, and very quiet.

Yankele would go out at night to the neighborhood peasants and buy food for his family. One night he heard from the peasants that the next night there would be a search for Jews hidden in the bunkers. Yankele did not say anything to the people in the bunker about the rumor. But the next night, instead of going out to get food, he sent his father. The Germans captured his father and shot him. The people in the bunker were wondering why Yankele sent his father instead of going himself as usual. But nobody would dare question him.

There were all kinds of rumors going around about it. Eventually when the war was over, all the people in the bunker survived except Rifka. She had a nervous breakdown. She suffered from a deep depression and severe anxiety. Yankele did everything he could to help her, but there was nothing that could be done for her. She was committed to a mental institution for an indefinite stay.

"Nu Chaim, what is your excuse now for not seeing them or trying to help them? There was no more shame. There were no people left to see your shame. Never mind. Don't answer it. Just listen.

"Meanwhile something terrible happened. Yankele became a policeman in the Russian police force. He was carrying a rifle one night while sitting in a movie theatre. He rested his arm on the rifle. Suddenly, we heard a shot and saw Yankele lying on the floor. As it turned out, it was his own arm that had accidently pulled the trigger and fired the rifle.

"Yankele was in the hospital, seriously hurt. He requested to see me. As I sat at his bed, he took my hand and spoke, 'Moishe,' he said, 'I want to tell you a secret. Something I never told anybody before. I think that the shot that almost killed me was a punishment for my sin.'

"'Sin, Yankele? What sin? I know that sometimes you like to take things that don't belong to you,' I said with embarrassment. 'That's not such a big sin to be killed for.'

"'No, Moishe, you don't understand. It has nothing to do with me being a ganif. I am a murderer. I killed my father. The rumors were true. I sent my father out that night knowing that he may be killed. Moishe, I want you to know that I don't feel guilty, and I don't regret what I did. I tell you this because I want you to know the truth.

"'You see, Moishe, when I was fourteen years old, I would work nights at my job. Many times, Rifka would beg me not to go. She was afraid to be home alone, she said. But I could not stay since my work could be done only at night. One time my friends did not show up for the job we had to do. So I returned home early. As I walked into my room that I shared with my sister, I saw my father in bed with Rifka, raping her. He was drunk. I wanted to kill him, but he was much stronger than me. I was afraid that he would hurt me and Rifka. All I could do is wish him dead.

"'When we were in the bunker, he would force himself on her any time he felt like it. My sister got more and more depressed. I could not do anything. Hurting him would mean disrupting all the other people in the bunker, and we all might get killed. So when I heard about the search, I sent my father, knowing that he could get killed. As I said before, I don't feel guilty. He deserved it. He destroyed his own child. Rifka would be better off dead than alive.'

"He closed his eyes and I quietly slipped out of the room. Yankele died shortly after.

"Well, Chaim, now that your investigation is over you know the truth. What are you going to do about it? Your dead nephew, from whom you were estranged all his life ... Who are you to judge him? Now, you are the one who should be ashamed."

Chaim turned around and, without a word, walked out of the room.

Being Ill

Some weeks ago, I went to spend a few days in Montclair with my daughter, Rosalie, and her family. The second day, I woke up with bad chills.

"Rosalie, please," I said. "Put up the steam. I'm very cold. I'm shivering."

"My thermostat is up over 75 degrees. It is almost 80 degrees in the house. You must be sick."

I took my temperature. I had 104.5 degree fever.

As both of my kids are doctors, they did not let me go home. They started to treat me with antibiotics. A day passed and nothing worked. I called my doctor. He told me to call an ambulance and go right to the hospital.

"You must be very sick since the oral medication isn't working, and 104.5 degrees is a very serious fever for an older person."

The ambulance came and rushed me to the hospital. After examining me, they told me I had a severe urine/bladder infection. I was given intravenous antibiotics and Tylenol Plus. This time the doctors told me I had a kidney infection.

The first day, nothing worked. I was still shivering, could not eat, and had diarrhea. All I wanted to do was sleep. I was put in a room with a woman who rang for a nurse all day, although the nurse never showed up. All night, she moved the bed rails up and down. It took seven days of torture until my infection cleared up. My poor husband, who stayed with me all day from 8:00 a.m. to 8:00 p.m., suffered with me.

My neighbor in the next bed was moved to a home. I was relieved, but not for long. The next day they brought in another patient. She must have been a little bit senile. She talked to herself all day and sometimes at night. I could not wait to go home.

Finally, after thirteen sleepless nights and miserable days, and weighing thirteen pounds less, I was released from the hospital. What a pleasure to go home. I thought, Now I will be able to rest and sleep as much as I desire.

The first day at home, I was woken up by an alarm clock. Near to me stood my husband, Sam, with a bowl of cereal.

"Molly, you need to eat a lot. You must get up and eat."

"But, Sam," I begged, "it is only seven o'clock!"

"You must eat! You lost thirteen pounds!"

Okay, I figured, I will eat breakfast and go back to sleep until lunch. That's what you think.

Two hours later, the shape of my husband appeared again. "Time to eat! You must gain back the thirteen." After two more hours, he gave me a glass of Ensure. It is a complete balanced nutritional drink that my doctor prescribed. I was to take a half a can three times a day. If you think that's enough, a few hours later I was woken up for a bowl of rice.

"Molly," Sam said, "you must eat. You still have some diarrhea."

Next came a slice of liver. "You are anemic. You must improve your blood count."

This routine was to go on until eleven p.m., when I got my last glass of Ensure. That was when I found out that my husband was cheating. He gave me three-quarters of the can of Ensure instead of half. He wanted to fatten me up in a hurry.

The second day went exactly as the first. I know that my Sam loves me very much. He is wonderful. A mother could not take better care of me, but sometimes too much parenting can turn to torture.

I felt I could not take much more of this treatment. I had to tell my Sam, "Please, stop!" I was going nuts! I was ready to throw the food on something or someone.

Then I got an idea to weigh myself. I gained one pound, but I told Sam four pounds (a little white lie). He was thrilled.

Now I said to him I could take care of myself, do everything for myself, thank you, my dear husband. I love you very much.

Brown

"It is brown. I am telling you, it's brown." My husband was saying it over and over with great energy. It began at the end of the 1930s in Poland. There was a fashion in shoes at that time called carioca. The shoe had white stitching all around the sole, with white laces and two large beads at the end of them. They were made by a special shoemaker and were very expensive. I don't know the reason why, but the carioca shoes were always made in brown leather.

My family was poor. We were six children without parents and could not afford a new pair of shoes for each of us every year. I always got the shoes from my older sister. Usually they were old and worn. As a child, I didn't mind it. But when I became ten years old, I wanted a new pair of shoes for myself. I was dreaming about brown carioca shoes.

My family knew how much the shoes meant to me. But there was no way I could get them. They were too expensive. Instead, they bought a cheap imitation, a pair of black rubber shoes that looked like patent leather with white laces and two big knots at the end of them. I felt terrible.

Somehow that incident made me very partial to the color brown. I think I was obsessed with it, but at the time I didn't know what an obsession was.

During the war, I took what I could get no matter what color things were. But as soon as the war was over and I came to the United States, I saw such a variety of things and colors, my obsession returned. Subconsciously, I would always pick something in brown: brown shoes, a brown hat, or a brown coat. Even in picking my children's or Sam's wardrobe, I was partial to brown.

My Sam was aware of my obsession. At that time, we were living in Brooklyn. A lot of clothing stores would display their merchandise in front of the store for passersby to look at. One such store was Woolrich. It was a men's store located next to a bank. They got a lot of business from the people who visited the bank.

One day my husband returned from the bank with a bright smile on his face. "Molly, you would not believe what I have in here," he said, showing me a plastic bag with something hanging in it. "Imagine, such a bargain! I bought a pair of brown pants for $10, half price! They are your favorite color, and, most important, they don't have to be fixed. They fit me perfectly!"

I didn't bother to look at the pants at that time. I just hung them in the closet with the plastic over them. I was very pleased that for once Sam bought something on his own since he never wanted to go shopping for himself.

On a Saturday night a few weeks later, we decided to go to a movie.

"Sam," I said, "why don't you wear your new brown pants?" I handed him a white shirt with brown stripes to match his pants—or so I thought.

Just before Sam was ready to get dressed, I decided to take a look at the pants. Maybe they needed ironing. When I opened the plastic bag, I was shocked. There I was starring at a pair of green pants, a bright olive green.

"Sam, what is this?" I yelled, pointing at the pants.

"What do you mean 'What is this?' It's my new brown pants."

"But, Sam, don't you see it is not brown? It's green."

"It is brown. I am telling you it is brown," Sam was insisting.

I didn't know if I should laugh or cry. I had just found out my Sam was colorblind.

The First Time I Heard the Word Shoplifter

WHEN MY CHILDREN WERE small but old enough to go by themselves to the market or candy store, they would tell me about their friends taking things in the store and walking out without paying. It was called shoplifting. They said it was a lot of fun. I told them that it really was stealing. They should never do it. They talked about it in a way that made it seem like it was a game. That somehow gave me the mistaken belief that shoplifting pertained only to children.

But I soon learned that things were different. It was not a children's game. Adults were involved in shoplifting too. My husband owned a butcher store with a partner. Some evenings, when the partner had to deliver orders, he would leave early. I would come to the store to keep my husband company.

One such evening, I walked into the store and saw a customer at the counter and my husband on the other side, cutting some meat. I had never seen the customer before and I am sure she did not know me. She must have thought that I was just another customer. I heard her saying to my husband that she did not like the way the cutlet looked. She wanted another one from the freezer. My husband left all the meat on the counter and went to the freezer. As he closed the freezer behind him, she turned with her back to me. I heard something drop into to her shopping bag. I did not know what to do. I could not check her shopping bag. It meant losing a customer. I got an idea. I went around the counter and started to move around the pieces of meat that were on it, pretending to wipe off the counter with a rag.

Soon my husband came out of the freezer. He looked at me as if to say, "What are you doing on this side?" He started to tend to the customer again. Suddenly he turned to me, saying, "Molly, there was a piece of flanken here. What did you do with it?"

"I don't know. I must have pushed it down while I was just trying to wipe up the blood from the counter. Let me go on the other side and look."

"I don't see it." I turned to the customer. "Maybe I pushed it and it fell into your shopping bag and you did not realize it. Let's take a look."

She looked and took out a piece of flanken. "You know, you're right," she said. "I would never have known until I got home. I would have called right away."

"I'm sure you would," I said. She was happy. We kept the flanken and did not lose a customer.

The Storm

THERE WAS A SMALL meadow, in the middle of nowhere, covered with grass and wild flowers, surrounded by trees whose branches seemed to reach up to the heavens. The sky above was deep blue, with tiny white clouds moving slowly across like little birds. A cool wind brought delightful breezes, causing the leaves to rustle. This, together with the singing of birds and the chirping of the crickets turned it all into a beautiful, whispering melody. A few feet away was a creek with water so clear you could count every pebble and see all the little creatures playing.

It was this meadow that we chose as a retreat from the heat in the big city. Along with a few close friends, we decided that this spot was an ideal place for a picnic. It started as a perfect day. The children played, getting along well. We were sitting around, talking, playing cards, and eating all sorts of delicious food that we had brought along with us.

I got very restless. My insides were shaking out of control. All I wanted was to go home and hide. Everyone thought that I was frightened of the oncoming storm that followed such stillness, but I knew differently. The stillness triggered a great anxiety deep within me. I remembered another such stillness, a stillness in a small shtetl in Poland that came before a pogrom. The streets were quiet and empty; the people were hiding. Not a living soul was to be seen on the streets. Nothing could be heard. It was stillness before a deadly storm—brought on not by nature, but by the Nazi murderers.

It took me a few days to calm down and get over the nightmares that tortured me. This was only one incident, but there were and will be others, which, like a curse, follow me throughout my life.

She Looks Exactly Like You

"SHE LOOKS EXACTLY LIKE you," was the comment of everyone who saw my daughter Evelyn for the first time. I personally did not see such a close resemblance. It wasn't until a particular incident occurred that I was convinced that people were right.

When Evelyn was eight years old, she joined the Brownies. In turn, I became a Brownie leader. On one of our trips, we took the Brownies to Idlewild (now JFK International) Airport. Evelyn got sick and had to remain at home. Since the troop had only two leaders, I had to go.

It was very difficult controlling twenty very curious little girls. I was glad when the day was over and we all settled into the bus and were on our way home. I sat in the back of the bus. Since I was very tired, I fell asleep, only to be awakened when the bus made a sudden stop. I opened my eyes and looked straight into the mirror in the front of the bus, and there she was, my daughter, Evelyn. I knew it was impossible. She was at home, sick in bed. It took me a few minutes to realize that the face in the mirror was my face. Just to make sure, I touched my nose and my eyes to see if the face in the mirror did the same. It was then that I realized how close our resemblance was.

Evelyn's personality as a child was actually quite similar to mine when I was her age. She was stubborn and very curious, doing things she wasn't allowed to, getting into mischief all the time … just like me!

A Simcha (A Celebration)

It was November 1944. The day was gloomy and nasty. The rains had just stopped falling. The weak autumn sun was trying hard to come out from under the thick clouds. The cold wind was blowing and shaking the raindrops from the remaining leaves on the trees. On that day, I was walking the baby that I cared for, trying to push the carriage hard against the wind that was pushing me back. As I came close to a railroad track, I saw a group of men digging ditches. They all wore Jewish stars on their sleeves. As I pushed the carriage over the track, the strong wind took off the hood of the carriage and blew it away! I just stood there helplessly, not knowing what to do. I was afraid to leave the baby alone in the carriage but I knew I must get the hood. At that moment, one of the men with the Jewish stars went after the hood and brought it back to me. I thanked him very much in Polish. He just shook his head and turned to the other men, saying in Jewish, "Look, such a skinny nothing little shikse has the right to live while our beautiful children are being slaughtered."

What could I say to him? I dare not tell him that I was one of them, that I had no more right to live than their children. That I was, maybe, more fortunate, fighting for my life without anybody knowing it. But I did not say a thing so as to not reveal my identity. I just walked away.

For a long time, this incident lingered in my mind and then faded away. After a great ordeal, I did survive the Holocaust and came to live in the United States. Here I was blessed with two daughters, Evelyn, the oldest, and Rosalie, the younger. When Evelyn started Hebrew school, she became very friendly with a girl named Sonia, whose parents also came from Europe. I never met them until Sonia's Bat Mitzvah. We were invited to the party. As I walked into the hall, mingling and talking with the guests, I felt someone staring at me. I looked up and saw a man gazing at me. I looked closer at him and suddenly I had a feeling that I knew him. I could not remember from where. The gentleman came over and said to me, "I am Sonia's father. I know you are Evelyn's mother but I know you from before. I saw you somewhere else."

We stood talking, asking each other questions. "Where were you during the war? Which cities did you come from? How did you survive?" Suddenly when he mentioned the city Zlochow, I remembered where I had seen him. He was the man with the Jewish star who helped the little shikse with the carriage cover. We both laughed and cried at the same time. It was hard to believe that after so many places and years, we came to the same city in the same neighborhood for one simcha.

An Overprotective Mother

BEING A HOLOCAUST SURVIVOR, I believed that my surviving the horrors and madness was partly a miracle, partly an answer to my prayers, and mostly G-d's hand leading me to the right place at the right time. The greatest tragedy that I lived through was after the war, when I found out that my entire family had been killed. This left me with deep wounds in my heart and a disturbed soul, but it did not destroy me completely. I was young and strong and believed that nothing could possibly happen in my life that could break me completely.

However, "Mench tracht und Gut lacht." I got married, came to the United States, and started a new life. We had two daughters. I turned out to be an overprotective mother. I watched over my children day and night. When they went to school, I would be in the window each morning waving good-bye, and I made sure to be there when they came home. When they became Brownies, I was a Brownie leader and then a Girl Scout leader. I got a part-time job while they were in school, and I would leave them with my husband at night while I went to college, making sure to get home in time if my daughter went out that night. Everything seemed to be going right for us.

It was the morning after my older daughter took her picture for the high school yearbook that the ground caved in under me. There she was, lying with her eyes wide open, without any expression, hardly able to say a word. We rushed her to the hospital. After countless tests, they told us that she had a virus from which her recovery was uncertain. My whole life came to a stop. I always believed that after what I had gone through during the Holocaust, I could never feel a deeper pain. This proved to be wrong. Fighting for your child's health and perhaps her life could take your own life away.

I quit my job, gave up college, and devoted myself completely to my child. I watched over her day and night. In time, she recovered, but something unpredictable happened to me. I was totally drained, both physically and mentally. I went into a deep depression. All I wanted to do was to lay in bed and be left alone.

My doctor told me that I was on the verge of a nervous breakdown and that I must get out of the house and be occupied. I could not go back to my part-time job as a bookkeeper or to college, as I could not concentrate on either. I took a job as a knitting instructor in a store around the corner from my home so I could walk there, as driving was too difficult for me at this time. I was not getting any better, until one morning I remember being in bed and telling myself, "Molly, you must get well. You know how much you love your husband and your children, and how much they love you. What is most important is how desperately they need you to take care of them. They need your guidance. They have no one else." I guess that moment was the turning point in my sickness. After talking to myself a bit more, I got out of bed, attended to my children, and went to work.

My recovery was slow. The knowledge of my family's love and desperate need of me proved to be the most important factor in my fight and made me even more determined to get well. It was a hard-fought battle, but with the help of G-d and my family's support, I won. I recovered completely. I survived. I am a survivor.

Treasure in the Attic

"MOLLY, MOLLY." MY HUSBAND was trying to wake me up. "It is late. If you want to clean the attic today, we have to start early." To tell the truth, I was not looking forward to the task, but I got up. After breakfast, we went up to the attic. When it came to cleaning, my husband and I had two different opinions. Sam wanted to throw everything out. I, on the other hand, liked to save everything, new or old. I felt it was close to a sin to dispose of things. We argued all the time. Things he put away to be thrown out, I would put back the minute his head was turned. We worked for a few hours, accomplishing very little. Sam got angry and left. I stayed, trying to open the big valise we had brought from Europe forty-five years ago. It contained the diapers, the little kimonos, and the receiving blankets from our older daughter, Evelyn. I did not remember putting anything else into it.

As I emptied the valise, I came across something very special, a treasure that I had been searching for, for almost fifty years. It was a piece of my dear, older sister Roza's coat, the only reminder I had of her. I took the remains of the coat, holding it close to my heart. When I felt something pointed pressing against my chest, I looked and there, in the pocket, I found a picture of a beautiful young girl: my sister, Roza. She was only twenty-eight years old when the Nazis killed her.

As I looked at the picture, tears streamed down my cheeks. "Roza, Roza," I kept repeating. "I hope you can hear me. I have so much to tell you ... how much I loved you and missed you all the years of my life. I miss your warmth, your love. When you were only twelve years old, you tried hard to replace our mother. You did. I felt like you were my mother. Now that I am a mother and a grandmother, I realize the hardships you endured, since I was such a spoiled child. Please forgive me. Your wisdom, your deep faith in G-d that you instilled in me, helped me to survive in the darkest moments of my life. You taught me how to cope with life's hardships. 'Molly,' you told me, 'when things go wrong, look down—not up. You will see somebody with bigger troubles than yours. Have faith in G-d, and He will help you.' Your words have guided me throughout my life. They still do. Good-bye, my dear Roza. I will never forget you. I will miss you for the rest of my life!"

Being Someone or Something Else

Despite the fact that I had no parents, I thought I turned out to be a normal, well-adjusted youngster. My family loved me, my friends found me fun to be with, and the teachers were happy to have me as a pupil. So I was pleased with myself. Rarely did I feel that I would like to be somebody or something else. If ever I did, it was just a passing fancy.

It wasn't until the Holocaust that I started to dream of being somebody or something else. I was jealous of every person who wasn't Jewish. I envied every bird, every animal that was free. I wished that I could be one of them. As silly as you may think it was, I wanted to be a porcupine. I was told that it is an animal that has a good self-defense mechanism. When you get close to him, his body gets covered with needlelike quills, so no one is able to touch him. I became obsessed with the thought. I used to daydream, pretending that I was a porcupine.

Some nights during a pogrom, I would wake up and touch myself, expecting to find quills all over my body. I knew that it was delusional, but when life gets so unbelievable that you cannot face it, your mind does not accept reality anymore. You start living in a make-believe world, where everything seems possible.

It wasn't until recently that I realized how deep an obsession can be.

One day a while ago, I came home from shopping, feeling very tired. I sat down trying to relax. I decided to meditate, something my daughter taught me. I let my body be completely still and my mind blank, just concentrating on one happy thought. Suddenly, my daughter Evelyn walked in. "Mother," she said, "I know you are meditating but I must ask you a question. What do you want to be?"

In my trance, I blurted out that I wanted to be a porcupine. "Mother, what are you talking about? I just meant if you and Daddy want to be first going up to get an aliyah or be the first to light a candle?" (She was planning a bar mitzvah for her son.) I came to and explained to her all about my obsession. "Mother," she said, "you must have been out of your mind." She is probably right. I must have been.

Newfound Friends

WHILE AWAY ON VACATION this summer, I had a most wonderful experience. We stayed in a small hotel named the Holiday, which is located in the Catskills and is surrounded by beautiful mountains and woods that spread for miles and miles. My husband and I are nature lovers, so we would walk through the woods each morning, admiring nature's beauty and serenity. We found one spot that we loved the most. It was a small creek. We would just sit on the rocks, listening to the rippling and splashing of the water over the pebbles and watching the tiny little fish and other creatures swimming around happily.

On one of these mornings, while watching the reflection of the sun's rays shimmering on the water, we noticed another couple sitting and watching. There was something very special about the way they looked at the water with eyes full of tears. I was very intrigued. I wanted to meet them, so I walked over and introduced myself.

Their names were Frieda and Ephraim Cohen. They were sabras, which means they were born in Israel. We started talking, telling each other about life in our countries. Frieda and Ephraim were soldiers in the Israeli army. They fought in the Six Day War, where Frieda was wounded. They were telling us about the hardships they went through and still do, the constant fear of violence and the economic problems. But in spite of it all, they made life in Israel sound like a paradise and spoke with such pride and love of the land. At one point, while talking about Jerusalem and Yom Kineret (Sea of Galilee), Frieda said with a special glow in her face, "When you stand by the Holy Wall or walk at night on the shore of the Yom Kineret with the stars above and the sea below, you are as close to heaven as you can ever get."

It was then that I understood why they looked at the water the way they did. It reminded them of home. They made me feel very close to Israel and to them. Suddenly, the two people who were complete strangers a short while ago became very special to me. We were the best of friends until the day they went back to Israel. We promised to write each other and hopefully visit in the near future. I am sure we will, because there is something very special that binds our friendship: our love for Israel.

My First Trip

I HAD BEEN BUSY for weeks, shopping for summer clothes, which are not so easy to find at the end of December. I visited a number of stores and boutiques in Brooklyn until finally I found the right wardrobe for my vacation. Then I spent a great deal of time fixing it. Shortening, lengthening, making some smaller, some a little bigger. Next came the packing. First I had to make sure that the valises were the right size and weight. For this, I got special help: my daughter, Evelyn. Since she had been on this vacation a year ago, she knew exactly what we had to take. She is a perfectionist. She made two lists: one for me and one for my husband. She listed every item that was to be put in the valises to make sure that nothing was forgotten. As we were packing, my friend, Bella, walked in. She was known to be a very envious person." I don't believe what I see," she said. "Everything so perfectly packed and Evelyn taking such good care of you. I wish I would be able to go and have all this help." I did not appreciate the tone of her voice but I was excited, too thrilled with the upcoming trip, to pay any attention to her. It was the first time that we planned a vacation in Israel.

The night before the trip, I woke up feeling itchy all over. I could not wait until morning. When I got up and looked at myself, I became hysterical. My body was covered with red blisters. I went to the doctor. He diagnosed my rash as an allergic reaction to a drug that I was taking at the time. He told me that this drug stays in the body for a month, which meant that my rash might last for a long time. Luckily, after two weeks of treatment with cortisone, my rash disappeared. But there was no way I could go on the trip. I was very disappointed. Although we went to Israel a year later … it was not the same. There was something missing: the excitement and thrill of the first time. Finally, my daughter and I decided that my rash and the cancelling of the trip was my friend Bella's fault. She gave me a *kina hora*, an evil eye.

No Escape

LIKE A ZOMBIE, I moved from one place to another, from one store to the next. I had no desire to shop. I knew that I was not going to buy anything. I just looked at the beautiful displays of spring clothes, but I hardly saw them. Like in a trance, I was pushing myself, "Go, Molly, go. Don't go home. Stay away. Don't go near that monster in your bedroom."

So I left the stores and walked around the mall again and again, going nowhere. It was getting dark. I knew I must go home. My husband must be very concerned. I made myself a promise that when I got home, I wouldn't go near the bedroom where the monster stood. But nothing worked. The minute I got home and took off my coat, as if by a magnet, I was drawn to the bedroom and hastily turned on the television: my monster.

What I saw and heard was nothing new. Just another attack on Israel. Some more soldiers killed in battle. How can I explain how these happenings torment me? How can I make somebody understand the deep fear and concern in my heart?

I don't claim to be more patriotic than any other American, or for that matter, any other Jew. No. My deep-rooted pain stems from my past. My frequent encounters with death make me identify with every soldier, every person being killed or tortured. I realize that my suffering will not help anyone. It can only destroy me.

So I turned off the television and ran again, this time to bed, hoping for a peaceful retreat. But I didn't find relief in sleep. My dreams turned to nightmares. I woke up shivering in a cold sweat.

I only hope and pray that this war will be over soon, and I will wake up one morning to a brighter day in a world of peace.

I Belong

"FASTEN YOUR SEATBELTS. WE are about to land." These words coming over the loudspeaker awakened me. It took a few moments for me to realize where I was and where I was going. I was on a plane on my way to Israel; my lifelong dream to see the Promised Land was about to come true. Another few bounces and another few sways and then the plane came to a halt. We landed at Ben Gurion Airport. Next we were taken by bus to the King David Hotel in Jerusalem. As I stepped off the bus, I went down on my hands and knees and kissed the ground of the Holy City. This was the city that every Jew of the Diaspora was longing for and hoped to see. I was truly lucky. I had lived to see it.

At first we toured Jerusalem and the nearby cities, and later the rest of the country. Every place we visited was sacred to me. I marveled at every stone and every ruin. Each one seemed to tell a story. Each one was a page of history. Just walking in the streets and seeing children play and talk in Hebrew, the language of our ancestors, was a delight for me. The first time I saw a group of Israeli soldiers, young girls and boys marching by, made me want to embrace each and every one of them. They were *our soldiers—Jewish soldiers*, and they made my heart burst with pride.

I was deeply touched by our visit to Masada, the legendary fortress, where the Jews chose to kill themselves rather than be captured by the Romans. On our return from the Masada, we visited some new kibbutzim and settlements. It was breathtaking to see the green fields and the small groups of trees that looked as if they sprung out of nowhere in the middle of the Negev.

The city of Tel Aviv made a great impression on me. Here was a bustling metropolis, with its modern shops, hotels, cafes, and nightclubs. We saw Jaffa, one of the oldest cities in the world. This port dates back to the beginning of civilization. The beautiful city of Haifa was located on Mount Carmel. The most wonderful thing to me was the welcoming of the Shabbat at the Western Wall. I felt just like my Israeli friend once told me, "When you are praying at the Holy Wall at night, with the stars above, you are as close to heaven as one can ever be."

As usual in the Jewish tradition, one cannot be completely happy, so I must confess to some very sad experiences on this trip. Visiting Yad Vashem, the memorial to the six million Jews who were killed by the Nazis, brought back some very painful memories. In some instances, as

I was looking at the pictures, I forced myself to close my eyes in order to be certain that I did not see someone close to me or a familiar face being led to death. I knew that an image like that would be impossible for me to shake. When I stood on the Mount of Olives, with its centuries old cemetery now partially destroyed, I could visualize another cemetery in a little shtetl in Poland with only a few graves left.

When the time came to go back home, I knew that I would always miss Israel very much. Seeing our little homeland made me very happy and gave me a deep sense of security. I now knew there was really a place where any Jew could return to—a home he could call his very own.

Changes

FROM BEING A NAÏVE little country girl, who lived a simple, sheltered, and fairly secure life in a circle of a very warm and close family, I was suddenly thrown into a world of chaos, confusion, crime, and death: the world of the Holocaust.

In order to survive, I had to change. I grew up almost overnight. From an innocent little girl, I became a shrewd, manipulating, cunning creature. I say, "Creature," because I did not act like a human being. I functioned and lived more by instinct than by reason or intelligence. It was the instinct of survival.

As the war ended, I arose as another being. The horrors of the Holocaust molded me into a bitter person full of rage, hate, resentment, anxiety, and, above all, an irrational prejudice. As time passed and my life took a turn for the better and my future became more secure, I started to build a new life with the man I married. My wounds started to heal and my anger subsided, with my anxiety being diminished. I grew into a more rational person. It was not until my two children were born that the deep emptiness inside of me, which was left after losing my whole family, was filled. I grew into my maturity. I became more broadminded, more realistic and much more tolerant of others, no matter who or what they were. I tried not to judge them. My growing up was so very painful that I pray that I do not have to face any more changes in my life or discover a need to grow any more. I would rather be a small person than have to go through this growth process again.

Decisions, Decisions ...

FROM MY EARLY ADOLESCENT life all I had to do was make plans-some unimportant, but some life-saving. I had to make up my mind which way to go, which turn in life to take in order to survive.

I was never stable in my decisions. I would plan to do one thing and then change my mind and do something else. I was just lucky that things turned out right for me. I always believed that my survival during the Holocaust was because of lucky circumstances or some kind of miracle rather than because of my planning or my decisions.

As I grew older, got married, and started raising a family, the difficulty of making up my mind became even greater. It was only eased by sharing it with my husband.

When my two daughters approached school age, my husband, being a religious man, wanted them to attend a yeshiva rather than a public school. But we could not afford a private school. He went to a few yeshivas, explaining our situation to them. He told them that we were survivors of the Holocaust and it was very important to us that our children have a Jewish religious education.

Everyone turned us down. I was very hurt by their lack of understanding and sympathy. So there and then, I decided, in spite of my husband's wishes, that I would not send my children to a yeshiva, even if I could afford it.

They attended public elementary school, high school, and New York city colleges, where they got degrees in their professions, in which they are very successful. But I was left with a guilty feeling. I believe that if they had attended a religious school and grew up to be truly religious, their lives would be much easier, more secure, and more peaceful.

It seems that for once in my life, I took a stand that may have been the wrong one.

Tradition

Growing up with only poor Jewish families, I wasn't exposed to many Jewish traditions except in our house. My thirteen-year-old sister took the place of a mother, taking care of five orphans. She tried to follow Jewish traditions as much as she could. She taught us the *Modeh Ani*, the morning prayer, and *shema*, the night prayer. She lit candles Friday night. But there was one thing that puzzled me. When I went into the house of one of the other Jewish families, they had lit four, five, or more candles, where in our house there were only two candles burning. "Why only two candles?" I would ask, but my sister never gave me a clear answer.

"You will find out when you get older," she would say. Growing up, I realized that my sister did not want to hurt me, reminding me that I had no mother, since only a mother could light more than two candles, one for each child. Somehow the lighting of Shabbat candles became an obsession with me. When I grew up and got married, I was overjoyed when Friday night came and I lit two candles. In time, I added more candles for each child. There were four candles burning in my candelabra. On every occasion I had, I would tell my children how important it is for Jewish women to light the Shabbat candles. It's the biggest mitzvah. I guess I was trying to instill in them the importance of tradition. In a way, I succeeded. When my older daughter, Evelyn, was about to get married, I gave her two candlesticks as a gift, so that she could light candles on Friday night. My biggest thrill occurred when she and her husband came for supper on the first Friday night of their marriage. I was about to light my Shabbat candles when my son-in-law came over and put his arms around me, saying, "Mom, would you please light another candle for me? You have another child, a son." Tears were rolling down my cheeks as I lit the fifth candle. In time, I lit one more for my second son-in-law.

Now, I have six candles burning in my candelabra. My two daughters follow the tradition and light four candles every Friday night—two for them and two for their children.

My efforts paid off.

Marine Marlin

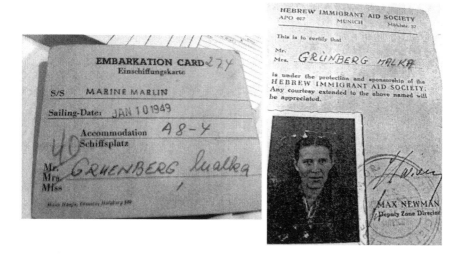

Embarkation Card 1949   *Molly's H.I.A.S. Identification Card*

Molly holding Rosalie and Evelyn 1954

Sam at his Kosher Butcher Shop
Brooklyn, NY

Molly and Sam
Catskills Summer 1955

Sam, Rosalie, Evelyn and Molly at
Evelyn's Sweet Sixteen October 1962

Molly, Aunt Esther and Sam
October 1962

Molly and Rosalie
Rosalie's Sweet Sixteen December 1966

Molly and Sam at Evelyn's Wedding
December 29, 1968

Molly, Sam and Evelyn December 29, 1968

Sam, Rosalie and Molly at Rosalie's Wedding August 25, 1973

Rosalie, Evelyn and Molly May 1976
Rosalie's Medical School Graduation

Molly, Evelyn, Sam, Jonathan and Toy Chanukah 1979

Molly, Sam and grandson Jonathan

Sam, Molly and granddaughter Elysia

Sam, Molly, Rosalie and Grandson Ryan New Years Eve 1986

Sam, Molly and Grandchildren Ryan and Elysia
December 1986

Evelyn, Elysia, Sam, Molly, Rosalie, Ryan and Jonathan
Chanukah 1986

Bubbe and Ryan 1988

Matthew and Bubbe Chanukah 1993

Molly and Sam
Catskills 1984

Molly and Sam at the JCC 1992

Molly being presented with writing award at Montclair State College

Molly Burak – Molly's Creative Writing Teacher

Status Seekers

OF ALL THE PAINS I ever had, the one I feared the most was a toothache. The thought of pulling a tooth always horrified me. It is not only the physical pain; it is the mental anguish caused by a memory of a dreadful experience of tooth-pulling during the Holocaust. Scared or not, you can't stop things from happening. At the time, we lived in Brooklyn, and I got a severe toothache. My dentist told me that when this tooth hurt again, I must go to a specialist to have a root canal or have it pulled.

As I was very nervous, I asked my daughter Rosalie to drive me. As usual, on the days that she didn't attend school she wore old dungarees and sneakers, both of which had seen better times. We parked in front of the dentist's office. Since there was still some time on the meter, I did not bother to put more money in. As we walked into the waiting room, the dentist was there. It looked as if he was waiting for me. "Hello, Molly. What is the trouble?" I told him and then introduced Rosalie. He nodded his head without even looking at her or saying hello.

I went into the office, and Rosalie remained in the waiting room. After examining my teeth, he said, "Molly, we will do root canal." I was relieved: no pulling.

"I think my daughter should put money in the meter since this will take a while," I said.

"Sue," he told the nurse, "would you tell the kid in the waiting room to put a dime in the meter?" The nurse came back saying there was still some time. As I was waiting for the Novacaine to take hold, he would not stop talking, telling me about his son the lawyer and his daughter the psychologist. Suddenly, he asked me, "What is your kid doing? Working and going to night school?"

What nerve this man had, asking me questions like this. "No," I said in an angry voice. "Rosalie is not working and not going to night school, or even college. She is in her second year at Columbia University Medical School."

His face changed. All he remembered to say was a long "Oh." For a while, he worked in silence. Suddenly, he turned to the nurse saying, "Would tell the young lady in the waiting room to put another dime in the meter? It may take some more time." What a switch, I thought. In twenty minutes, Rosalie changed from a *kid* to a *young lady*. As if that wasn't enough, as I was leaving, saying, "Good-bye, doctor," he replied, "Good-bye, Mrs. Greenberg, and say hello to your lovely daughter."

Mrs. Greenberg, I repeated in my mind. What happened to Molly? It was always Molly. What kind of a game is this man playing?

I was angry. As I got in the car, Rosalie asked, "What's wrong, Mommy? You look very upset." I told her what happened. "Mother, don't pay attention to people like him. They are called status seekers. It is all in a day's game for them. They don't judge you by your true values, your inner qualities: honesty, intelligence, and decency. They are only impressed with more external things: wealth, position, and power."

Anti-Semitism

OUR LIFE IN EUROPE was one long struggle with anti-Semitism. Leaving there and coming to the United States, I believed that we left behind us all prejudice and discrimination. Soon I found out how wrong my beliefs were. In this country, I was again faced with anti-Semitism on a few occasions.

The first time was shortly after we came to America. We rented a two-room apartment on the fourth floor. As we were moving in, the super started questioning me. He asked me where I came from and what my name was. When I told him that our names were Molly and Sam Greenberg, his facial expression changed. "I hoped it would be something like Sykorski or Jaworski." As I found out later, he was Polish and very anti-Semitic.

In time, we met many people from all walks of life, backgrounds, and origins. Most were broadminded and understanding, but some displayed their anti-Semitism in sneaky little ways.

I used to play cards with a group of women in the neighborhood. We were six girls: three Jewish and three Gentile. One time during the game, while talking about shopping, one of the non-Jewish girls made a statement. "You heard?" she said, "there is a new store opening on 86th Street. That's all we need is another Jewish store in Brooklyn." That was the last time I played with them.

Another incident happened very recently. I decided to get a job. My manager was a blond, tall, and handsome man. I did not know his nationality, but I found out pretty soon as the snake of anti-Semitism started to creep out.

At first he started to tease me. When I came in in the morning, he would ask me, "Did you have a bagel and lox or gefilte fish for breakfast?"

"No," I answered. "I had bacon and eggs."

One time a customer came into the store. To be truthful, she was a little difficult, but my manager overreacted. He insulted her saying that he did not care for her as a customer. He asked her to leave the store. As she left, he turned to the other sales girl in the store, saying, "She is one of them who invaded Livingston. All summer they spend in the Catskills, all winter in Florida, and in between, they come here and annoy our people." Then, if that was not enough, he turned to me and said, "She is your landsman (your countryman)." That did it. I quit my job soon thereafter.

Germs

"MOTHER, HOW COULD YOU?" I heard my daughter Evelyn's voice. "You see Toy sniffing all over the floor." Toy is our little dog, a Toy poodle.

At first I did not realize what she meant. "What did I do?" I asked.

"What did you do?" she said in a voice that suggested that I committed some terrible crime. "You gave Elysia a piece of bread that fell on the floor. It must be full of germs. She could get sick!" Elysia is my little grandchild. I did not know what to say. My daughter Evelyn's floor is as clean as anyone's table. At that moment an incident came to my mind about eating from the earth's soil.

"Evelyn," I said, "let me tell you a story. In 1942, when the Nazis invaded Poland, they made ghettoes so that the Jews would be concentrated in one place, making it easier to destroy them. One day we learned that there was going to be a pogrom. My family and I fled from the ghetto to the woods, where we hid in a bunker. We stayed there for four days. We had very little food and no water. As we were becoming dehydrated, we decided that one of us should go out at night, leave the bunker, and bring back some snow. Since I was the smallest one, it was easiest for me to crawl out and hopefully not be seen. I went out late one night, being very careful to make sure that no one could see me. It was pitch black. I took some snow, put it into a pot and crawled back into the bunker. To make sure that I did not leave any footsteps, I crawled backward, shaking the snow off of the bushes to cover my tracks. As I was putting the snow into my mouth, I realized that it tasted very salty. I knew what it was and so did the others. A dog or some other animal had urinated in the snow. Knowing that did not stop us from eating the snow. No one got sick or even nauseous. For us it was a lifesaver!"

Ruthie

I MET RUTHIE WHILE standing in line next to her as we were waiting to get dinner in a community kitchen in the displaced persons camp, Fohrenwald, which was in Germany. We introduced ourselves. It felt like something clicked between us. We became instant friends. After getting dinner, we promised to meet the next day in the nearby park. We met. We talked. We cried. We had a lot in common. We were both the same age, both came from a small shtetl, and both left without a single living relative except our husbands: my Sam, and Ruthie's Max. We were both pregnant. Our children were born one week apart. I had our daughter, Evelyn, and Ruthie had a son, Steven. That made us even closer. We were always together. People called us the war sisters.

When Evelyn was a year old, I became very ill. I woke up with a terrible backache. I was rushed to the hospital, where I was diagnosed as having a severe kidney problem. I might need an operation, they told me. An operation. I thought I could really die. I became very upset. After surviving the Holocaust, I thought there was no death for me. My biggest concern was my baby. What was going to happen to her? Who would take care of her when Sam was busy? I became quite hysterical.

A day before the operation, Ruthie came to visit me. We talked, I cried, and she cried with me. Suddenly it dawned on me. Why not ask Ruthie? I knew that it was not the thing to do. But when you are dying, everything is right. "Ruthie," I said, "I'd like to ask you a favor and please don't say no. Will you take care of my baby if I die?"

"Molly, what are you talking about? You are not going to die. You will live. You will be all right in a few weeks."

"Please," I begged her. "Promise me."

"I promise," she said.

Thankfully, a few days later my body passed the kidney stone on its own, so surgery was no longer needed.

One thing could be said about my relationship with Ruthie. It's like there was always a competition, and she needed to be on top. After the surgery scare, Ruthie didn't let me forget our agreement.

She made me feel indebted to her. Unfortunately the time came when I had the misfortune to pay her back. How very much I wish I did not have to do it. If G-d would only leave things the way they were. Carrying the feeling of debt was much easier than the pain of Ruthie's tragedy.

Ruthie had two sons, Steven and Jerry, and one daughter, Pauline. I had two daughters, Evelyn and Rosalie. Her younger son, Jerry, was a brilliant student. He was accepted to every Ivy League college: Harvard, Yale, Princeton, Columbia, University of Pennsylvania, and Cornell. He picked Yale because his girlfriend was there.

A few months before Jerry's graduation, his girlfriend broke up with him and married someone else. Jerry did not complain; he did not say a word about it to his parents. They went to his graduation. He graduated Magna Cum Laude. They begged him to come home for a while since he was on vacation, but he refused. When Ruthie came home, she told me that after he kissed her good-bye and started up the hill on the way back to his dormitory, he turned and waved good-bye. She felt like her heart stopped for a minute.

On a Sunday afternoon two weeks later, a policeman knocked on my friend's door. "I am sorry," he said. "Your son Jerry is dead. He drowned in the lake next to the school. Nobody knows if it was an accident or a suicide." How could anybody describe the anguish of my dear friend?

After that, I spent every free minute I had with Ruthie.

In time, she started to recover and tried to go on with her life. I was really happy for her. But G-d had something else in store for her. Eight years later, Ruthie suffered a complete nervous and emotional breakdown. One minute she would cry, "I want to go to Jerry." The next minute, she yelled, "I don't want to die." She would not take antidepressants or sedatives. She claimed that neither helped her. Eventually she had to be hospitalized. She refused to go voluntarily, and so her family had no choice but to make the decision for her. After a month's stay in an inpatient setting, where she received therapy, medication, and shock treatment, Ruthie returned home. She seemed better but was still left with a void that could never ever really be filled.

Riva
Heavens Weep and Angels Laugh

THE ROAD WAS WET and slippery. The heavy rain and thick fog made it almost impossible to drive or see more than ten feet ahead. My daughter, Evelyn, was the driver of the car. My husband and I were the passengers in the back seat.

We all kept quiet, each deep in his own thoughts. We were on the way to a funeral of our very close friend, Riva. At eighty-eight years old, she was the oldest person from our shtetl. It was not the death of an old person that we were all mourning. It was the death of the mother of all the people in our shetl who survived Hitler. It was the death of a martyr.

Once, Riva was a beautiful woman married to a man who worshipped her. They had six children: two girls and four boys. The youngest was a month old when the Nazis occupied Poland. In one year's time, Riva lost her husband, two sons, and a daughter. She was left with a ten-year-old son, an eight-year-old daughter, and an eight-month baby girl. The family hid in a bunker with some other Jewish people. Riva was told to get rid of the baby because her crying could attract the attention of the Gestapo and they could all get killed. Riva was faced with an impossible decision. She could not destroy the baby and she could not leave the bunker. In order not to jeopardize the lives of her children, one night she took her baby and left her on the steps of a church. She never knew what happened to her.

When the war was over, she heard some rumors that someone had found the baby on the steps and took her home, but she died soon thereafter.

Riva never found peace in her heart. She thought that maybe she was alive somewhere and she couldn't find her.

Surviving the war with her two children, she left the shtetl and went to a displaced persons camp in Germany, and then to the United States, where she had brothers and sisters who helped her start a new life.

Just as she began to adjust to her new circumstances, fate handed her another blow. One day she received a notice from a Jewish organization that they captured the Nazi who killed her oldest son. They wanted her to provide witness testimony. Even though it was very hard for her, Riva decided to go to Germany to participate in the hearing. What she experienced there broke her up completely.

The courtroom was filled with Germans. The Nazi soldier denied everything, claiming he never killed anyone. Riva's arguments that she saw him shoot her son in cold blood were in vain. The defense attorney argued that there were no grounds to sentence his client since it was her word against his.

When the judge read the verdict of "not guilty," the crowd in the courtroom remained silent. Riva told me that she felt like they were ripping apart her newly reopened wounds.

Time does not heal everything but it does mend it to some degree, as it did Riva's wounds. She went on with her life. Her children grew up, got married, and gave her grandchildren. Riva never found happiness in life, just some contentment. When she was eighty-eight, she got very sick, never recovered, and died within a year.

After hearing some very moving eulogies, we left the funeral home. On the way to the cemetery, it still rained heavily. However, when we reached the cemetery, the rain tapered off. Suddenly, as the casket was about to be lowered into the grave, the rain stopped completely. It looked like the clouds parted and the sun started to shine. It seemed as if the heavens were crying for Riva as long as she was on earth, but the minute she was put to rest in her grave, the angels received her with smiles of sunshine.

"Good-bye, dear friend. May your soul find peace in heaven since your life was hell on this earth."

A Surprise Party

"THIS IS WHAT I call real nachas," my friend Bella was saying. "Imagine a young boy like your son-in-law, Amos, a child of refugee parents, being honored by the city for his work as a prosecutor." As a rule, I never brag about my children. As a matter of fact, I don't even talk about them. Not that I am so modest; I am just superstitious. I am afraid of a kina hora, an evil eye. But this time I could not help it. I told all my friends about the party: the people with whom I worked and even people I just happened to know. I was a little puzzled that everyone seemed to know about it before I told them. I figured my big-mouth friend, Bella, must have talked.

My daughter Evelyn, Amos's wife, was very interested in making sure that no one would spill the beans. My husband, Sam, and I were not allowed to come to visit her for three weeks. She knew that her father likes to talk, and she told me she didn't want to take a chance on him spoiling the surprise for Amos.

My younger daughter, Rosalie, took me shopping at a very exclusive boutique. She made me buy a dress that I thought was a little too much for the occasion. But … Rosalie insisted that I must be very well dressed.

Finally, Saturday, the day of the party arrived. We had to get there 7:30 p.m. before Amos showed up at 8:00. Rosalie picked us up at 7:00, which was late since the ride from Brooklyn to Livingston, New Jersey, takes a minimum of forty-five minutes. As we came to the Goethals's Bridge, Soly, Rosalie's husband, suddenly remembered that he was supposed to call another doctor to tell him something about a patient before he left the hospital. We had no choice but to search for a pay phone. I got very upset as it was late, but I did not say a word. Of course it took ten minutes to find a working phone that he could use.

Soon we were back on our way to Livingston. As we approached Evelyn's house, Rosalie let out a scream. "Mother, you won't believe this but my dress got caught on my high heels and the hem got ripped. Let's stop at Evie's house so you can fix it."

That did it! "I am not walking out of this car," I yelled. "It's 8:30. Everybody is there already but us. It will take another fifteen minutes to get to the hall. We may as well go back to Brooklyn. And take a look at the house. It's dark. Nobody is home. How can I fix your dress even if I want to?"

"No problem, Mother. I have a key to Evie's house."

"Okay, okay. I will fix it," I said, "but please, Rosalie, remind me never to go with you to any surprise party again."

As we opened the door, all the lights went on in the house and there they stood: all my family and friends from Brooklyn, and many other important people in our lives, yelling, "Happy Thirtieth Anniversary." My Sam and I just stood there flabbergasted. As I looked at him, I saw tears in his eyes. After a while, I opened my mouth, wanting to thank everybody, but all that came out was a sob followed by a hysterical cry. It was the first party ever given to me in my life. Like a little girl who never outgrew her childhood, I was thrilled with every wish and every gift I received. It was a night that I will cherish forever.

Nachas

NACHAS IS A WONDERFUL feeling. Having nachas is like collecting a reward for something we did. It is being gratified for our efforts. We get nachas from a lot of things, but the most important one is nachas from children and grandchildren.

All parents do their best trying to bring up their children to be good human beings. But life is sometimes very cruel, and no matter how much we give of ourselves, how hard we try, things don't always work out the way we want or plan. So often, parents get only heartbreak and trouble for their efforts. Seeing that makes me realize how very fortunate my husband and I are.

Our two daughters grew up in a very difficult time—the time of Woodstock, hippies, and flower children, when drugs and permissive ways were the style of living. Our children survived the pressure of outside influences and grew up to be fine people. We have a lot of nachas from them. They are married and gave us three wonderful grandchildren. Watching our grandchildren grow up is the greatest nachas of all.

Zayde

I HAD NO PARENTS, no zayde, and no bubbe. I sorely missed having parents. I was especially envious when my friends told stories about their bubbes and zaydes: how they would play with them, bring them gifts, hug and kiss them. I used to make up stories, telling my friends, "My bubbe and zayde live far away. They can never come to see me."

The problem was that the more stories I told, the more I started to believe that they were true. It was much later, when I was older, that I realized that the stories I told were nothing more than childhood fantasies.

It was the time when Hitler invaded Poland, where we lived. He ordered pogroms, murdering our people in cold blood. As cruel as it may seem, a lot of the time, I thought that my parents and my bubbe and zayde were lucky to be dead. They died a natural death in their own beds, not in a gas chamber or from bullet wounds, left to bleed to death or to be burned alive.

I survived the Holocaust. In time, I met a wonderful man who soon became my husband. We had two daughters, Evelyn and Rosalie, who grew up and got married. Each had two children. Finally, my husband and I became a bubbe and a zayde.

I never saw my husband display as much affection toward our children as he did to the grandchildren, rolling on the floor with them and telling them stories. Three of the grandchildren are now older. They don't want so much cuddling or attention. They would pretend to have a cold as an excuse to shy away from being kissed or hugged.

However, my husband is a lucky zayde. We have a fourth grandchild, Matthew, who is three and a half years old. He worships his zayde, and zayde adores Matthew. As Rosalie, his mother, says, "They have a love affair." Every time I call my daughter, Matthew picks up the receiver and asks to talk to his zayde.

Their conversation is short. Zayde says, "I love you," and Matthew answers, "I love you too. When are you coming? Bring bagels and lox." (We usually have breakfast together on Sundays.)

A little while ago, Matthew left his red jacket in our house. I put it on a hanger and hung it on the bedroom doorknob. Every time zayde passed the door, he would stop and tenderly caress the jacket, saying, "Mein Mathewlle."

But the most touching thing is seeing the two of them together. When zayde holds Matthew, his face shines with such happiness, he looks as if he were holding a precious treasure in his arms. And little Matthew clings to his zayde, looking at him with sparkling eyes, full of love and trust. Seeing them together like this brings tears of joy to my eyes.

Sometimes I think that the fact my husband and I survived the horrors of the Holocaust and lived to become a bubbe and a zayde is not just G-d's blessing—it is a miracle!

Longnose

THERE ARE A LOT of people who I like to call on the phone for one reason or another. If I were to be left with only one call, the call I would like to make is to a baby too young to understand what I would want to say. He is a five-year-old child. It is my grandson, Matthew.

It happened two years ago:

My husband, Sam, had to go to a doctor in New York City. I did not feel well at the time, so my daughter, Rosalie, volunteered to take him, leaving me with her housekeeper, Jackie, and little Matthew.

As they were leaving, Matthew, went over to his mother, saying, "Mommy, don't worry. I will take good care of Bubbe." After they left, little Matthew came over to me and said, "Bubbe, please lie down on the couch. I will give you something that will make you feel better." He ran to his room and came down the stairs with his Longnose elephant that he loved more than anything else in the world. With tears in his eyes, he placed it on my chest, saying, "Bubbe, I know you will get better. You see how happy Longnose is! You have nothing to worry about now. You can go to sleep. He will watch over you. You will wake up happy." Then he went to the housekeeper and asked her to give me tea so that I would fall asleep. And I did.

When my husband and daughter returned from the city, they found Matthew sleeping next to me on the couch, holding his arm around my arm. When he woke up, he ran to his mommy, saying, "Mommy! Mommy! Bubbe is all right! Longnose helped her! I took good care of her ... but I ... I think I will let her keep Longnose." Then he sighed. "It is only an elephant. I will get another pet."

Tears were running down both his cheeks ... as well as ours.

That was one of the greatest gifts that I ever received.

A Career Choice

"I THINK IT IS time for you to turn off the television set and get back to your studies."

"Bubbe, why must I study?"

"I guess you have to if you want to become somebody," I responded.

"I could become somebody without studying."

"Like what?"

"Like what? Well, I could become a truck driver ... and that's what I am going to be. So I don't have to study!"

"Ryan, I think that you have a wonderful idea. You chose the right occupation. Imagine driving in the middle of the night, in darkness and snow and blizzards. It must be so exciting!"

"Bubbe, it won't work. You are trying to scare me but I am not afraid of darkness or anything else. I made up my mind. I will be a truck driver."

"That's good, Ryan. I am proud of you. But I think you should also have something else, like a profession, just in case the trucking business doesn't work out."

"Bubbe, there you go again. I know what you're thinking, but you're afraid to say it. Because you know I hate it. I don't want to be a doctor like my daddy and mommy. I don't want to have a beeper that beeps every time me and daddy try to have some fun."

"I did not mean that, Ryan."

"Oh yes you did. Everybody does."

"Ryan, I think you don't want to study anymore today. How about taking a shower and going to sleep."

"Okay, Bubbe, but would you stay with me? It is kind of dark in my room."

In no time my macho truck driver was sound asleep, holding onto me so tight.

Labels

LABELS, LABELS, SO MANY labels. There are two large bags of clothing, and each piece needs a label. I always enjoyed seeing the clothes and doing the labels. So what disturbs me this time? I should be thrilled, because this year both of my grandchildren will be going to sleep-away camp. I should be happy. In a way, I am, but something is troubling me. Is it the loss of another year? It seems like just yesterday I was sewing labels, and now I have to do it again. Where did the time go? Do the years get shorter as we grow older? Do the months and the days pass quicker? I wish time would just stand still. Everything seems to be so right just now. I don't want any changes, any new experiences, any surprises. I know that my wishes are not realistic or rational, but what do wishes and feelings have to do with reality or reason? So I sit at my sewing machine and sew labels. The rhythms of the machine distract the flow of my thoughts, but not my feelings. My eyes get misty. From time to time, a tear flows down my cheek and a label or two gets wet. I don't know why I am crying, or maybe I do.

Nature's Laws

LIKE THE FLICKERING OF a candle that is about to go out, her child's breathing was getting weaker and slower. At times, it seemed like it was gone, and then it would pick up again. She would not let anyone near her ailing little one. It seemed she wanted to be alone in her despair. Suddenly, the newborn's tiny body started to shake and then stretched out, and his breath was gone forever.

There were no tears in the mother's eyes, no crying, just a howl so sad that it tugged at your heart. She cleaned her child, washed it, and then pushed it off the bed, letting nature take care of him, turning herself to her other healthy child.

We called her Snowie because she was as white as snow, with two beautiful black eyes. She was about one foot long—a toy poodle. She was my daughter Rosalie's junior high school graduation gift. Snowie was a happy and playful dog. She learned all kinds of tricks and loved to take long walks. When Snowie was four years old we mated her. She had two puppies. One was healthy, and one died a few short minutes after it was born. After giving birth to her offspring, Snowie was never the same. She stopped being playful and could not walk much. We found out that she had angina. She died in my hands when she was only seven years old. She had a heart attack.

Was her illness a mere coincidence or was it brought on by the birth of her child? Who knows?

Nature.

Starting All Over

LIKE MOST PARENTS WHOSE married children lived in another state, we wanted to be close to them. Since we had no other family except for them, it seemed like a great idea, especially when our children begged us and insisted that we had to move.

I personally was very reluctant to take such a big step at our age. But with my husband and the children insisting, I lost. We moved from Brooklyn to New Jersey—to West Orange, to be specific—leaving all my friends and my work. The first few weeks were very busy and exciting: fixing up our apartment, buying some new furniture, and trying to organize our newly redesigned lives. Also spending a great deal of time with our children and grandchildren seemed to make time pass quickly—at least at the beginning.

A few months passed, and I suddenly started to get very restless. I felt bored and lonely. I missed my friends, my job, and my house. In short, I missed Brooklyn very much. There I was in a strange town, not knowing a soul except for my children.

Where do you go? How do you meet new people? At our age, how do you make new friends? Someone suggested that we join the West Orange Jewish Community Center.

So we did. The problem was that when we went there, we were introduced to the wrong group of people who attended the center. They were all considerably older than us. Some were just sitting there playing cards, while others were just talking. We tried to talk to the card players, but they weren't very responsive to us. For a brief time, we just sat there listening to the conversations, which revolved mostly around peoples' family and children—how good some were or how badly they behaved, how brilliant their grandchildren were, sheer geniuses! But all of them seemed successful. I felt these people lost who they were somewhere along the way and were now trying to create an identity for themselves through their children. I felt very sorry for them, and at the same time got a little upset imagining myself at that stage of life. I wasn't ready for this environment. I just wanted to go home; so we did.

But ... we came back again and again because we had nowhere else to go. After coming back a few times, we met another group of people, though not that much younger than the others, but they were full of life and vitality. We discovered people participating in all kinds of activities:

dancing, singing, art classes, and more. I grew to really admire them and their spirit for living life. I also met some highly intellectual people who were interested in politics, all kinds of scientific discussions, creative writing, and more. How exhilarating!

Subsequently, I joined a creative writing class. I truly enjoyed it. I found it so interesting and very stimulating. Finally I met some very nice people with whom I shared common interests. We became very friendly, but that is another story.

The people I got to know at the JCC were among the most interesting individuals I had ever met. They came from all walks of life. Everyone, including me, was trying to express themselves by putting their feelings, their beliefs, and their experiences down on paper. Not one of us was a professional writer, but some were more talented than others, and some were truly outstanding. The nice thing was that although some were more critical than others, they all appeared very supportive and helpful.

The most wonderful person in the group was our teacher, Molly. She never criticized our creations. She corrected us but never pointed out faults in our writing. In the worst stories, she would always find something she considered very good, something which she could praise.

Without a doubt, Molly was the most understanding, most giving, person anyone could ever meet: a wonderful lady and a great human being!

A Little Bit Better, A Little Bit Bigger, A Little Bit Longer

LAST SUNDAY, WE HAD special visitors from Brooklyn: my best friend, Sonia, and her husband, Max. We came on the same boat from Europe. Since then, we developed a friendship. Sonia is a lovely person. She is bright. Her husband, Max, is intelligent and has a good sense of humor. She only has one fault. Everything that is hers was still, "a little bit better, a little bit bigger, and a little bit longer."

When we got our first apartment, I was very excited. I told Sonia that my living room was twenty by fifteen feet long. Her answer was, "That is nice, but mine is about two feet longer." When she saw my carpeting, she thought it was lovely, but hers "was a little bit thicker. Your feet sink when you walk on it." When we went shopping for clothes and bought almost identical dresses, she would examine mine and say she thought that her material was of a better quality. Since then, we called her, "Sonia with the longer thing."

Anyway, we were happy they came to visit us. We had a lovely time. I prepared a delicious lunch of homemade salads. I even made potato latkes, since I knew Max favored them. For dessert, we had homemade apple pie and coffee.

After lunch, we just sat around and talked, reminiscing about old times: how hard it was in the beginning with little children and a small income, how few toys our children had, and how poorly we dressed. In time, things got better. Our husbands opened their own businesses and became successful. Each of us bought a house and furnished it nicely, and we became aware of how to dress better. We would look at labels and buy designer clothes. We bought shoes by Gucci. Unless you owned a pair of Gucci shoes, you did not count. Thirty-five years ago, his shoes cost fifty to seventy-five dollars. Now, we agreed, we just buy what feels and looks half decent, never noticing labels.

While talking about dressing, I made a remark that "my daughter Rosalie is a very good dresser. She wears mostly tailored designer clothes. Her profession requires it." No sooner had I finished talking when guess who walked in: my Rosalie, in a pair of dungarees with a hole on each knee, with a man's flannel shirt that looked like she slept in it at least two nights in a row, a pair of sneakers that had seen better times, and hair that looked like she just walked out of the shower—but with a happy, bright face.

Sonia gave me a look of disapproval that sent shivers down my back. "So this one wears designer clothes," she said. Rosalie, who knows Sonia very well, just gave her a bright smile. "You see, Sonia, these are my weekend and holiday clothes. I am so happy when Saturday comes and I don't have to wear the sleek suits and dresses. I feel free. My body breathes through the holes in the dungarees. And my hair takes a rest from the blower and curlers. It's a great feeling."

Sonia ignored the explanation completely. She turned to Rosalie and said, "My Anita (her daughter) would never wear anything like that. She is a lady. She dresses well." Rosalie just ignored her. But I got very annoyed that after all these years, Sonia had not changed and had not grown up. Hers was still "a little bit better, a little bit bigger and a little bit longer."

Parents and Children

ANNA IS SITTING NEXT to me, in a small shul, in her senior housing residence. She hardly ever opens her prayer book, and her expressionless eyes are staring into space. The only time she shows any emotion is when the rabbi reads the part of the Holy Torah that tells us, "Honor your father and your mother." Anna then closes her eyes, and tears roll down her cheeks. She never speaks to anyone.

Suddenly, one Saturday she turned to me and whispered, "I have to talk to someone. Please, will you listen to me?" I nodded, and she spoke. "You know, Molly, I am living alone in this senior citizen home. I feel lost and deserted. I have only one son, Lenny. He brings me food and other things I need, but he never brings himself. I want to tell him how lonely and hurt I am, but he does not have the time to listen. He tells me he can't be bothered. He has his own family to take care of. Who am I? Suddenly, I am a stranger!" She started to cry.

I did not know how to console her. Then I recalled a story I had once heard from a wise old man. I told her the story.

Once there was a mother bird that had three babies. One day she sensed that a violent storm was approaching. She knew she faced a difficult task, carrying her children across a turbulent river to save their lives. She took the oldest baby and started on her way. It was a foggy and rainy day, making the flying treacherous. Halfway across the river, she stopped and asked her baby if he would go through a similar hardship for her.

"Sure I would, Mother," answered the bird. Without a word, the mother dropped the baby into the river and flew back for her second one. She then asked her second baby the same question. His answer was even more reassuring. "Mother," he said, "I would do anything for you." The mother dropped the second baby into the river.

Finally she went back for the youngest bird. She asked him the same question. "Mother," he replied, "I don't know if I would do the same thing for you, but I know I would definitely do it for my baby." The mother bird carried her youngest across the river to safety.

When I finished my story, Anna smiled at me. She said, "I understand what you are telling me. Our children don't owe us anything; they have to look after their own children."

I was pleased to cheer her up, at least for a while. However, my happiness was soon shattered by doubts. I began to wonder how I would face the challenges that old age brings. Would a simple example like the one I gave Anna be sufficient for me? How would I cope with the obstacles I might encounter?

I am a Holocaust survivor. I have been left with wounds in my heart that never heal and disturbances in my soul that will never go away. Despite the ordeals and tortures that I have endured, I consider myself a fortunate person. My survival was a miracle, and my later life has been filled with G-d's blessings.

I grew up in Europe, where an old mother was placed on a pedestal and was considered a family treasure. Will I be able to accept today's contemporary family structure, where an aging mother becomes a burden and has to live alone, even if it is against her will?

I have two wonderful daughters. I know that if I ever have to be alone, they will take good care of me, physically and financially. I will never be cold or hungry. But what about my starving soul? When nightmares of the past torment me through the night and shadows of my lost loved ones haunt me through the day, when loneliness creeps into my wounded heart, I know I will yearn for my children's closeness—a kind word, a warm embrace to assure me that I am not alone, that I am still loved, needed, and wanted. Will they be there?

Regardless of what does happen, I also know that when I approach the challenges of old age, I will be able to meet them by not dwelling on my misfortunes, but instead by being aware of my many blessings.

Outraged

SUNDAY IS OUR SHOPPING day. In the morning, we do food shopping. In the afternoon, we go looking for clothes. I don't necessarily buy, but like most women, I touch, I try on, and then I go to another store and compare prices. Last week I went to an outlet store named Daffy Dan's. As I was browsing around, I heard a baby cry. I turned around and saw a little boy about three years old crying hysterically. I asked him his name, and he said, "Jimmy." I tried to comfort him, but he never stopped crying. He was screaming, "Mommy! Mommy! I want Mommy!" He would not go with me to the desk, so I asked a woman who passed by to please go and tell them at the desk to announce on the loudspeaker that there was a lost little boy named Jimmy.

It took a long time for the mother to show up. She was a young, pretty girl carrying a bundle of clothes in her arms. I tried to tell her that it's dangerous to leave a little child alone in a store like this. "Shut up!" she said to me. "It is my child. I do as I like." If that wasn't enough, she dragged the crying child and started to hit him.

"Stop it!" I said. "Why don't you comfort him instead?"

"Butt out!" she said. "Why don't you mind your own fucking business!"

I was outraged.

It Seems To Me

I OFTEN WONDER WHAT is happening to the family structure in our society. Where is the closeness, the tight-knit relationship between mother and daughter? It seems to me that family ties are becoming looser and looser, and sadly closer and closer to the breaking point.

Why is this happening? Whose fault is it, the parents' or the childrens'? Are the mothers and fathers responsible for it, trying so hard to make the children independent, trying to keep them close by all the wrong means, giving the children all the material things they want though not necessarily need, but not giving them enough of themselves? Or are the children responsible when they try to leave their parents as soon as they are able?

It seems to me the greatest responsibility lies in the upbringing of the child by the parents and by society. From infancy, the child is taught to be separate from the mother, to be independent of her. Often it is because the mother works, but even if she does not, she just wants to be free. The infant is left with a baby-sitter who is usually a responsible person, but she is not the mother—a physical substitute, not an emotional one. The baby-sitter cannot give the child the deep feeling of love and care that a mother can. Maybe the child feels the lack of a mother's closeness and love and becomes insecure and rejected in his early life.

As the child grows older, he faces even more obstacles. He is shuffled from one place to another. First to preschool, then to nursery, to kindergarten, and so on. By the time he reaches high school, he has been shuffled around, in and out, many times. All this is done in the name of independence and progress. Then comes the big step, college, often out of town, which gives the parents more freedom. But what about the youngster? It seems to me that many of them are not ready for the complete separation from parents and home. He goes anyway, because it is the thing to do. Often the youngster cannot adjust to the new environment and becomes more and more insecure, which, in some cases, can lead to deep depression and even suicide.

After surviving college and getting settled in marriage, a career, and family involvement, the young adult finds the scene reversed. His parents may become a problem. They do not live with the children since they might interfere with their privacy and freedom. So the children do exactly what was done to them. They give their parents the material things they need and some financial support, but very little of themselves. The cycle of shuffling restarts. First, it is a community for older people, and then hotels for senior citizens, and finally old age homes. In some cases, when only one parent remains, it is very difficult for him to be alone. An older parents needs the closeness of children but was trained to believe he has to be independent even if it means loneliness and unhappiness. It is the thing to do.

It seems to me that we pay too high a price for our so-called independence and progress. We are losing something very important, very special: the closeness, the warmth, the security of an old-fashioned home and family. By no means do I suggest regressing. I just think we should not progress at so fast a tempo—by revolution—but rather at a slower pace—by evolution.

Always a Mother

Always a Mother

BY MEMORIAL DAY WEEKEND, May 1995, it was clear to Mom and the rest of the family that she was getting much weaker. She was running out of energy in her brave fight against the unremitting cancer, which marked the last years of her life.

As the most recent scans indicated that the cancer had spread to her liver, Mom spent Saturday, May 27, in the hospital ambulatory surgery center getting a special catheter placed in her chest. The oncologist explained that she had run out of usable veins for blood draws and chemotherapy. Lying in recovery, she looked so tired and worn. Ten years of struggling with breast cancer can do that to you.

Then by mid-June, the inevitable happened. Mom became too weak to walk without assistance. Within a few days, she didn't have enough strength to feed herself and needed help going to the toilet. Her voice and body grew stiller. Within five days in this weakened state, she lapsed into a coma. Her last coherent, conscious words were Sunday evening, June 19. My sister's son, Jonathan, was going to sleep-away camp the next morning, and he had come to see her before he left. "Good-bye, Jonathan," she said. Over the next few days, my sister and I took turns keeping vigil at our parents' house. One or both of us kept Dad company, helped care for Mom, changed her adult diapers, and just stayed beside her as she lay in bed in her own world. Sometimes she called her dead brothers' and sisters' names as she lay in this twilight state. "Mendel. Rubin." But the rest of what she said was too hard for us to understand.

We would try to talk to her as if she were really there and heard us, but sometimes it was just too sad. There were moments I couldn't help but feel like a fool, telling jokes as I was near her so maybe she/we would feel less morose and could deny the reality before us.

By Thursday, we had a hospital bed set up in the living room (an ironic name) to make it easier to move around and care for Mom. The hospice nurse came and said someone in Mom's state could stay alive for as long as another week even though she wasn't eating or drinking. I found that hard to believe.

As Thursday wore on, her breathing became more labored. I knew that time was running out, so I decided not to go home that night. I slept in my parents' bed, and Dad fell asleep on the living room couch. I did not want Mom to die during the night and she and Dad be all alone.

Friday, June 23, was a busy day. My sister had to take care of some things for her daughter, who was going to camp the next week, and I had to take time to take care of business for my family. During the day, Evie and I took turns doing our activities so that our parents would never be without one of us present.

It was Friday evening, at around 7:34 p.m., and soon the Sabbath would start. It began later than most other times of the year, as it was just after the summer solstice. Mom's breathing became more noisy and irregular. Evie and I went to look at her and see if there was anything we could do to make her more comfortable. Mom was just lying there, eyes closed, her breathing more labored and intense. My sister stood on one side of the hospital bed, holding her right hand, and I was on the other side, gently caressing Mom's left hand. This was the first time the three of us were in physical contact all day. We were telling Mom that we loved her (although doubting anyone heard us except each other and Dad on the other side of the room). Suddenly as we were holding her, a single tear rolled down her cheek from one of her closed eyes, and her breathing abruptly stopped.

Evelyn and I looked at each other in disbelief. If I didn't know better (and maybe I don't), I would have sworn that my mother cried as she had to say good-bye to us, her daughters.

Mom died around 7:38 p.m., less than a half hour before sunset. Because the Sabbath had not yet begun, we were able to reach the rabbi by phone, just as he entered the synagogue, and discuss having a funeral

Sunday morning. Had it been twenty-five minutes later, the Sabbath would have begun and the rabbi would be unable to talk on the phone, therefore making funeral arrangements a much more complicated process.

The memorial service and burial was on Sunday, June 25. Not only did my mother, Molly Feuerstein Greenberg, take exceptional loving care of her family during her life, but even in death, she still wanted to make things a little easier for me and my older sister, Evelyn, and our dear father. Even the moment she chose to take her last breath could not have been better timed.

AT AGE SIXTY-EIGHT, A year before she lost her battle with breast cancer, my mother wrote the following story, titled "A Child's Prayer."

A Child's Prayer

I WAS BORN IN a little village, Gusztyn, in eastern Poland. I was an orphan raised by my older brothers and sisters. We were poor. Although we did not starve, our meals were plain and scarce. But when the holy holidays came, I not only had the best of everything to eat, but I also got a new dress and new shoes.

On Yom Kippur, the holiest day of the year, every Jew fasted and prayed for good health, parnose, and, most important, to be inscribed in the Book of Life. For us, the young children, it was a happy day. While the adults were fasting, we indulged in all kinds of goodies. Dressed in my new dress and shoes, I walked around radiant, stiff like a peacock.

In the morning, all the children played outside the shul. At eleven o'clock, everyone went inside to hear the rabbi speak. After finishing his speech, he asked all the children and the adults whose parents were still alive to leave the temple before Yiskor started. Yiskor is the name of the Jewish prayer for the departed. I was the only child who could stay. I felt very special.

I sat next to my sisters. When the rabbi started the Yiskor prayer, I suddenly jumped up and ran to the bima (the pulpit) where he was standing. "Rabbi," I said, "I want to say Yiskor for my mommy and daddy, but I don't know how."

"Can you read the Yiskor prayer, child?" he asked.

"No," I replied. "But I know the Modeh Ani (the morning prayer)."

"Okay. Let's say the Modeh Ani," the rabbi said.

When we finished the prayer, he put his hands on my head and said, "May you be blessed from G-d." Then he turned to my family and the people in the shul. "This child just did the biggest mitzvah that one can do," he explained. "I knew her parents. They were good, religious people. But even if they had been murderers, burning in hell, this child, with the prayer, just paved their way to eternal rest in heaven." When he finished, everyone's eyes were misty. I hoped that I helped my parents achieve the peace that they deserved.

As for me, I know that I was blessed. I survived the Holocaust. Though the wounds in my heart, after losing my entire family, never healed, they did mend. In time, I got married and had two daughters, who grew up to be good, decent human beings and gave me four wonderful grandchildren.

Now that I am losing the battle against cancer, which has tortured me for years, and I am facing death at any time, I don't complain. I just thank G-d it is me and not one of my children. I don't despair. I know that when the time comes, I will not die from a bullet or knife wound like my brothers and sisters, but in my own bed or in a clean hospital bed, surrounded by my children and grandchildren. I am blessed.

At the memorial service, all I had to do was read her words aloud. Leave it to my mother to write her own eulogy!

She summed up her life with brevity, yet great poignancy and spirituality. Even in death, this was one last task she took from her children's shoulders. My father, sister, and I have never stopped being aware that it was really us, the family that she created, that was truly blessed by having such a wonderful, loving woman in our lives. As my six-year-old son, Matthew, said to me at her funeral, "I thanked G-d for Bubbe; she was a gift." Amen.

My father, Sam Greenberg, was also a member of the Senior Creative Writing Class at the JCC. He too wrote about his experiences living through the Holocaust. My father's faith and ability to still love despite what he experienced is something that I admire and hope that I emulate.

Sam Greenberg's Story

It was March 1944, the beginning of the end of the Hitler regime. I, my father, my sister, and twenty-one other people were hiding in a bunker in the woods. We had made the bunker from a bomb crater. The morning was beautiful, and the mood in the bunker was quite happy. We had heard the Russians were getting closer and closer to our city, and we were hopeful that our salvation was not more than two weeks away.

Suddenly, my father decided to leave our bunker. He wanted to wash his hands in the snow. The cover of the bunker was made mainly of branches and leaves so that it would not be noticeable to the Gestapo. However, the moment he lifted it, he saw a few Gestapo and several Ukrainian policemen. He tried to crawl back into the bunker, but it was too late. The Gestapo had seen him. As my father attempted his return, the police started shooting into the bunker and ordered the people to get out. When nobody moved, they took heaps of straw, ignited them, and threw them into the bunker. My sister and I came out, but my father refused to leave. He would rather suffocate than get shot.

The police placed us in a line and started to shoot. My sister received the first bullet. She fell to the ground and then picked herself up and begged me, "Shulim (Sam), save me!" I could not help her. She was shot again and again.

The Gestapo then gave me a stick and made me mix the burning straw

161

and push it down into the bunker where my father was choking from the smoke.

Suddenly, I recognized a policeman who I knew from before the war. I told him that I had a lot of gold and money hidden in the city. If he would take me there, I would give it all to him. He agreed. All of the other people were killed.

It was bitter cold. I walked barefoot in the snow for five kilometers until we reached the city. I had no money and was only buying time. Suddenly, the policeman became suspicious, and he pointed his rifle at me. He said he was going to take me to the cemetery and kill me.

I knew then that I was going to die. The cemetery was located at the outskirts of the city. To get there, we had to cross a small bridge. As we reached the bridge, I turned and jumped into the river beneath it. The policeman fired at me several times, calling out my name. I did not move. Believing that I was dead, the policeman went to find someone to remove my body from the river.

I wasn't sure if I was alive or dead. I started to feel my body. I was able to move my hand and my legs. I was alive! I got up and ran into the woods.

Three weeks later, the Russian army liberated us. My town had consisted of two thousand Jews. Now only one hundred and fifty were still alive.

I returned to the bunker where I had left my father and my sister. His dead body was half burned. All that was left of my sister was her blond hair and a few bones. The rest of her body had been eaten by wild pigs. I took both their remains, put them in a coffin, and said Yizkor (the Jewish prayer for the deceased) for them as I buried the half-empty box so that they could rest in peace. May their memory be a blessing.

Sam and Molly
May 1992

3 Generations at Grandson Jonathan's Bar Mitzvah May 1992

Miracles

The World is Full
of Wonders and Miracles;
but we take our hands
and cover our eyes,
and see nothing.

~Israel Baal Shem Tov

Printed in Great Britain
by Amazon

47547380R00111